YOUR FUTURE, YOUR DREAMS:

HOW TO RETIRE ANYWHERE IN THE WORLD

Angie Brimer

ISBN: 9798523984877

Contents

Reviews

Reviews and feedback help improve this book and the author. If you enjoy this book, we would greatly appreciate it if you could take a few moments to share your opinion and post a review on Amazon.

1. Introduction

Retirement is the goal for so many of us. While some people cling to jobs as a source of identity, others long to see the day they can leave their work behind and retire to a simple and relaxing life.

We work tirelessly and give a piece of ourselves to the jobs we hold. When we finally choose to leave our working lives behind, we deserve to retire in the way we want. While most people choose to retire in the same city, state, country they've known all their lives; others retire overseas and trade in their daily routines for adventure.

More and more Americans are starting to see the benefits of retiring abroad and are intrigued by the prospect of a new life. Leaving behind your old routine and the life you've known is scary, but it can also be exhilarating. Of course, moving out of your hometown is a deeply personal, and somewhat painful, experience.

I remember leaving the bustling city of New Delhi for the comfort and beauty of tall skylines peppered with beaches and palm trees. My move to Singapore was a scary one; I was terrified of leaving behind the friends I grew up with, the smells I had grown accustomed to, and the memories I had created.

Singapore did, of course, become my home for many years. I made new friends, new memories. I loved living in a country where the beach was as close to you as the mall was. A country that was as rich in culture as it was in money. A country where the food court at the mall was as gourmet as any 5-star restaurant. I fell in love with the culture, the colors, the smells, and the vibrant nature that made this country what it was.

There are so many reasons to move to a foreign country, and the point in telling you my story is that no matter how scary this move might be, you will grow to love the place you move to as much as the place you moved from. Maybe even more. You will create new memories, find a new favorite restaurant, learn a new language, and learn more about yourself than you ever thought possible.

The most important thing before retiring overseas is to make sure you're doing it for the right reasons, and having those reasons clearly laid out in your mind. If you're not committed to the idea of moving abroad, chances are it won't work out. Commitment doesn't mean there shouldn't be any feelings of fear or sadness, it simply means that in your mind the good outweighs the bad and you feel ready for this move.

It's also important to outline your retirement plan. As you'll learn in this book there are a number of great countries you can move to depending on your preferences. In some places, you'll be able to drastically elevate your standard of living by indulging in things such as a cook, a gardener, even a full-time maid. In other places, you'll be so close to the ocean that you'll taste the salt in the air. No matter where you choose to go, this book will show you how to create a home away from home.

I personally have traveled to over 20 countries including South Africa, France, Spain, New Zealand, Russia, and Greece. Additionally, I have lived in Singapore, India, Tokyo, and I currently live in New Jersey, USA. So take it from someone who's traveled the world, you can make a home pretty much anywhere.

The experience of living somewhere new will shape your thinking and bring a certain flair, cultural sensitivity and authenticity to your worldview. Adapting to a different cultural environment is not nearly as difficult as it may sound, and this book will guide you through the necessary steps to properly adjust.

A change in scenery and culture is just one of the many reasons people choose to retire overseas. Other common reasons include better weather, retiree incentives, a lower cost of living, or making a reality out of a dream.

One of the most popular reasons that people choose to retire overseas is the allure of a lower cost of living and access to affordable healthcare. A lot of countries have a far lower cost of living than the U.S and this will be discussed in detail in chapter 4. These countries also tend to have access to more affordable healthcare than the US does, as will be detailed in chapter 8.

There's emotional reasons to retire overseas and there's also logical, pragmatic reasons. But no matter what your reason is, it's a decision you can't go wrong with as long as you've thought it through and done the appropriate research. This book is a great starting point for your research — it'll guide you through the logistics, the emotions, and the steps to retiring overseas.

When you've spent your entire life working a 9-5 job, you probably didn't take the time to explore the world and create new memories. Many people see retirement as the time to finally do that. You're at a place in your life where responsibilities are shrinking and you want to enjoy the freedom that you've earned. You can enjoy this freedom in the mountains, by the ocean, or in a big city with twinkling lights. It doesn't matter where you do it. What matters is that you enjoy it, and are at peace with it.

Your freedom begins now; how will you spend it?

2. Logistics and Residency Options

Retiring overseas can present itself in a number of different ways. You can use this time to travel the world and see all the places you couldn't see when you were working. Either because of time or money constraints. You could also choose a couple countries every year and divide your time in those places; these would be places that you've deemed special or homey in some way. Another option is to just live overseas part-time, and retire to warm, sandy beaches in the cold, harsh U.S. winters.

There are so many ways that you can choose to spend your retirement overseas. Some people even choose to pick up a part-time or freelancing gigs to earn some income in retirement in order to support their overseas retirement dreams. You can carry these part-time and freelance gigs with you wherever you choose to go in the world, as long as they're remote and can travel with you.

The fact remains that there are so many ways to spend your retirement and if you do choose any of the plans outlined above then you don't really need to address the question of residency. However, if you are planning to retire in one country and make this specific country your home then you need to plan and strategize your options early on. First and foremost, you'll need to pick a country that offers a path for becoming a legal resident.

A great starting point for this process is to hire an attorney to help formulate a list of possible countries that you can retire in. This list should comprise of all the countries that offer a legal path to residency, and the ways in which you can become a legal resident. It's important to create this list prior to house-hunting or falling in love with a place. Your attorney can also help process any paperwork and forms for the visa that you choose to apply for. There are a number of different visas and different paths to residency, depending on the country you'd like to live in.

In the 1980s, Costa Rica decided to capitalize on American retirees and started a program to help lure in expats looking for a retirement destination. They started the very first program to target retired people and called it the pensionada program, more commonly referred to as the "retired visa program". You qualified by simply meeting a minimum amount of retirement income. If you were able to meet this amount, then Costa Rica granted you the right to live in their country for as long as you pleased.

Since the genesis of this retirement visa, many other places have created similar programs. These places include Ecuador, Panama, Uruguay, Colombia, Belize, the Dominican Republic, Argentina, and Mexico. American retirees bring in a lot of money, making them a huge commodity, this is why so many places are targeting Americans with these retirement visas. They're all trying to attract people like you, and in doing so they're offering amazing incentives and benefits! These benefits will be highlighted in chapter 11.

Countries in Europe also offer retirement visas for Americans; these countries include Ireland, Portugal, Spain, and the UK. All of these countries have varying requirements for their retirement visa, but the primary qualification for all is a minimum amount of retirement income/ pension.

Many people choose to move to these idyllic locations, which is why these types of retirement visas were created in the first place. However, another common route that retirees take when looking to settle in a foreign country is finding a country that offers residency in exchange for an investment. These investments are usually in the form of real estate or through starting a business in the country and stimulating economic growth and creating local jobs.

Your attorney can help you file the appropriate documents and they can also detail suitable options for investments. They can also help break through legal jargon and explain things to you in a more clear, cohesive, and casual manner. Additionally, your attorney will also help you process your visa for whatever country you're choosing to reside in.

Of course, you can start the process by entering your desired country on a tourist visa; this is useful for scouting houses and getting a feel for the place. Eventually, once you're committed to a specific country — your lawyer can get the ball rolling on either a residency visa or permit for the country where you'd like to be a legal resident. Once you've received permanent residency, you're allowed to live in the country for as long as you'd like and go in and out as you please. I highlighted some options above for Europe, Central America, and South America. But if you're looking for a complete change of pace, you can even look into residency options in Asia.

The three countries in Asia that makes it easiest for Americans to retire are the Philippines, Thailand, and Malaysia. The Philippines has a two-way road to gain permanent residency. The first option would be to go through the Philippine Special Resident Retirees Visa (SRRV). You qualify for this by meeting a minimum amount of retirement income. If you're able to meet this set amount, then the Philippines will grant you the right to live in their country for as long as you want. The other option is to invest in the economy of the Philippines. Usually the investment required is around $20,000 USD.

The Philippines is a beautiful retirement haven! Picturesque, sparkling-blue waters and white-sand beaches on the outskirts and tall skyscrapers in the cities. This country has everything. Expats fall in love with the food here and they all rave about the number of exotic islands and cool mountain towns there are to explore. An increasingly popular place to retire, The Philippines should be near the top of your list.

Thailand is another very popular option in Asia and many Americans choose to settle down here. The warm, palmy weather juxtaposed with opulent palaces, temples, shrines, and beaches that run for miles, make this a great destination to retire. Rich in culture, good food, and relaxation, Thailand is a massive hotspot for foreigners. Thailand's only requirements for retirees is that you show a set income (typically around $25,000 in your bank account) and you must be over 50 years of age.

Malaysia is another popular destination for American retirees; to live here on a permanent basis, you can apply for what's called the "My Second Home" Program. To qualify for this program you need to show about $2,500 USD in annual income and have about $90,000 USD in assets. Malaysia is a beautiful place to live; unlike some other countries in Southeast Asia, Malaysia energetically encourages foreigners to live here! The cities in Malaysia offer a wide range of options in entertainment; from opera to symphonies to bars and clubs with lively music. Malaysia is rich in culture and has a number of museums, galleries, and temples to show for it. There's also a diversity in activities here, from trekking to boating to scuba diving and exploring nature reserves, Malaysia has something for everyone!

No matter where you choose to take up residency, it's important to remember that you're a legal resident of this country, but not a citizen. This is an important distinction to note; as a resident, you don't necessarily have the right to work. If you would like to work in the country you're living in, you'll most likely need to file for a work visa.

In addition to the distinction between residency and citizenship, it's also important to note the two different types of residency visas. If you have a permanent residency visa then you can live in the country for as long as you please. With a temporary visa, you typically need to renew the visa every couple years. After renewing this visa a few times, you can typically apply for permanent residency.

Distinctions like these are very important to note in order to abide by the proper rules set forth by the country. This is another way in which an attorney is incredibly beneficial; they will help run you through the proper procedures and proper course of action for visa applications and such things. The last thing you want to do is mess up your visa application or note down something inaccurate. Additionally, your attorney can also help you better understand the process, and expedite certain bureaucratic processes.

The majority of countries I've listed in this chapter will have a few prerequisites in addition to meeting a minimum income requirement. These prerequisites will most commonly include a physical exam, proof of local health insurance, and in some cases — an FBI report stating that their are no legal charges to report. In regards to the income requirement, the countries I've listed require a monthly income/ retirement pension between $600 to $3,000 USD depending on the country. In most of these cases, the income you get from your Social Security is enough to qualify on its own.

It's also important to remember that some of the countries I've mentioned in this chapter will allow you a path to citizenship. If this is something you're interested in, your attorney can guide you through the process of naturalization, which will happen after you complete the residency program set forth by the country of your choice. Sorting out your residency visa should be number one on your list. It's the perfect stepping stone to a seamless, simple, and serene retirement abroad.

3. Where to Go? The Most Popular Places To Retire

Now this is the fun part! Perhaps the most fun part of the entire process, but it's also the most crucial. Where you decide to settle down will dictate the entire tone of your retirement.

It would be a complete shame to hype something up in your head, fill out all the long, tedious, necessary documents, only to land in the place and realize this is not at all what you had dreamed up in your head! This is why I highly recommend visiting the place you plan to retire in before committing to anything. When I say "visit" I don't mean a week — I mean something closer to a month, maybe even two.

Living in any place for a month will give you a general idea of what living there longterm would look like. You may think the beach is for you until you realize the humidity isn't for you at all. You may love the idea of a sleepy town until you realize the town itself is lulling you to sleep when all you crave is excitement and adventure. Our reality often has a way of not living up to our expectations; to avoid this let-down, we need to prepare as much as possible. A big part of this preparation is visiting our ideal destination and making sure that it is in fact — "ideal".

While creating our list of ideal destinations for retirement, many of us wonder about the most popular places to retire. At the very top of this list, I of course have to put, Portugal. Portugal is ranked as one of the best countries to retire in the world. It›s ranked high for a number of reasons; some of which include great housing, healthcare, and cost of living.

Portugal is without a doubt one of the most popular spots for Americans to retire. You can find a huge expat community all over Portugal; but especially in Lisbon, Algarve, and Cascais. Portugal is one of the safest places in the world; that, combined with it's tropical weather and fun vibe, make it an immensely popular retiree destination.

The beaches here are fresh out of a movie — clear blue waters surrounded by sandy white tapest ry. With beaches like this and views of a gorgeous stretch of the Atlantic coastline, it's no wonder Americans are pouring in to Portugal. They're welcomed with sunny weather and pine and oak trees coating almost every inch of land.

Portugal also has great health care, which makes it a super desirable place to retire. Much like all of Europe, Portugal has a socialized health care system. And the biggest selling point here is that Portugal gives you access to this health care system when you become a legal resident. I'll discuss health care in more detail in chapter 9; but for now, all you really need to know is that socialized health care is the most coveted type of health care. It basically means that the government provides any and all aspects of health care for you. This includes employing health care providers, running health care facilities, and paying for all its citizens' healthcare.

In addition to its excellent healthcare Portugal also has amazing sites, cliff-top vistas, a great record when it comes to safety, prime real estate, and a fair cost of living. Portugal also has what's called a Golden Visa Program, enabling Americans to easily retire here, provided they make a qualifying investment in Portuguese real estate. All these reasons and more, make it one of the most popular destinations for American retirees. If swimming, sun-tanning, boating, and lying on sandy beaches is what you're looking for then Portugal may just be the spot for you!

Second to Portugal would be **Panama**. Panama is another very popular spot for Americans to retire. One of the major points that works in Panama's favor is it's extremely low cost of living. American retirees can peacefully live in Panama while spending less than $3,000 USD a month. This includes utilities, rent, groceries, and even entertainment. Panama is also fairly close to the US making it easy to fly home for the holidays or even just on nostalgia trips.

Just like Portugal, Panama also has incredibly affordable health care, a reliable metro-system and inner-city buses, amazing infrastructure, and well-paved roads. All that paired with its ocean views and warm weather, make it a total hub for American retirees!

As I mentioned in the previous chapter, Panama has something called the pensionada program; more commonly referred to as the "retired visa program". As an American retiree, you qualify for this program by having a pension of at least $1,000 USD a month.

Once you're approved to be a part of this program, you can live in Panama for as long as you please!

Panama boasts a very cosmopolitan menu. They've mastered every cuisine you can think of, so when you're craving a little bit of home you're all set to go and won't be disappointed! They have restaurants all around the country that specialize in Indian, Peruvian, Italian, Japanese, and Cambodian food. Their supermarkets are packed with cheap local produce, as well as imported products that hail from all over the world.

Closely following in Panama's footsteps is **Costa Rica**. Another very popular destination for American retirees. Great waves coupled with a balmy climate and rich culture make up this beautiful country. Its low cost of living and friendly locals make it both a beautiful and desirable place to retire.

The name Costa Rica literally translates to "rich coast" in Spanish. And this name is as accurate as ever. Costa Rica is the perfect haven for the tired and the weary; it's beauty is so astounding that even the most skeptical travelers would fall in love with this country. Costa Rica's sandy beaches are as white as chalk and the water here is the most beautiful shade of aquamarine. Waterfalls, forests, and beaches run rampant in this country and if you are looking for a tropical safe haven then look no further.

As I mentioned in my last chapter, Costa Rica was the first to start a targeted program for retired people called the *pensionada* program. You qualify for this program by proving that you have a monthly income/ retirement pension of about $1,000 USD. If you meet this requirement then you will be given a temporary residency permit, that you can renew every 2 years (provided you still meet the requirements).

Costa Rica is safe, peace-leaving, has affordable medical care, and a wide range of real estate options. Couples can peacefully live (albeit not lavishly) within a range of about $2,000-$2,500 USD a month. This price is all-inclusive; so rent, utilities, groceries, healthcare, transportation, and entertainment are all factored in. Costa Rica is truly a home away from home, a jewel to behold, a slice of paradise. All this makes it one of the most popular destinations for American retirees.

Mexico is next on the list. A supremely popular destination for Americans. Versatility is key here — you can live in a small fishing village, or a little city in the mountains, along the pacific coast, or even in a big cosmopolitan city. Mexico's Pacific Coast is one of the most accessible "overseas" destinations for American retirees, which is why Mexico has earned a top spot on the list.

There's already a developed expat community in all parts of Mexico, so assimilating and fitting in would be a fairly easy task for you. There's also a bunch of affordable options for real estate across Mexico — some of these areas are Playa del Carmen, Cabo San Lucas, Tulum, Puerto Vallarta, Ensenada, and San Miguel de Allende.

You can apply for a temporary resident visa in Mexico as long as you qualify under one of the following criteria:

1.) Can show a monthly income/ retirement pension of about $1,400

2.) Own property in Mexico with a value of $210,000 or more

Mexico is the perfect spot for you if you're looking to fly the nest but not fly too far! It's also the perfect escape for warm weather and cheap living.

Another country with a fairly low cost of living is **Colombia**. Colombia is a very popular place to retire for American citizens because of its beauty and low costs! With mountains coming together with big cities and the sea, Colombia is a safe haven that welcomes all retirees. Rick in culture, rich in food, rich in color, and rich in adventure, this country is the perfect place to retire and it already has an established expat community.

With pastel buildings lining the streets and greenery so lush that the forests look like a fairytale setting, Colombia's beauty is unparalleled. Rich in biodiversity, Colombia is flushed with butterflies, poison dart frogs, pink river dolphins, and cotton-top tamarins. There's even a wide range of flowers, including orchids and magnolias that run rampant across country lines. Their oceans are no different — filled with every type of freshwater fish you can imagine; each representing a different color of the rainbow! A haven of biodiversity, Colombia has over 50,000 species of plants and animals; making them the second most biodiverse country in the world.

If nature is your kryptonite and scouting different types of plants and animals is something you enjoy then Colombia might be exactly what you're looking for! You can apply for a retirement visa in Colombia, as long as you can show a monthly income/ retirement pension of about $800 USD. This is definitely one of the cheaper alternatives, compared to other countries requirements.

Ecuador is another cheap alternative, and only requires a monthly income/ retirement pension of about $800 USD for a retirement visa. Ecuador is one of the most popular places that Americans choose to retire. Often times the rosy picture we paint of a life abroad, surrounded by art and beaches, isn't an accurate representation of reality. However, in the case of Ecuador, it is 100% accurate! Ecuador is filled with beauty, culture, and adrenaline-fueled activities — you can trek the Inca Road, catch the perfect wave in the infamous Galapagos Islands, raft through Montane Forest, and paraglide in Crucita, all while admiring the landscape of the Pacific Coast.

Ecuador is as fun as it gets and is an ideal retirement setting for active couples that are looking for fun and adventure with a beautiful, water-front backdrop! It's not all fun and games in Ecuador, as the country also has a rich culture that weaves its way through every city, village, and mountain-top.

Traditional festivals in Ecuador are a big expat favorite. The festivals pay homage to past ancestors and the indigenous people that once inhabited this beautiful country. These types of festivals are flooded with traditional music, rituals, food, and attire.

Many Americans choose Ecuador for the cultural immersion, others choose it for its fun and beauty, but most choose it for its low cost of living. A couple can comfortably live in Ecuador for about $2,000 USD. That's less than the cost of rent for one month for an apartment in Northern Jersey! $2,000 will get your far in Ecuador — not only will it cover your rent, but also your utilities, food, transportation, and entertainment for the month. This low cost of living is a massive draw for expats, which is why Ecuador is so high on the list for American retirees.

Another country high on the list for is **Malaysia**. Malaysia is one of the most popular places that Americans choose to retire in Asia. This is due to a number of reasons from the low cost of living to the phenomenal cuisine to the tropical weather to the beautiful beaches. Malaysia is an excellent option if you've always wanted to live in Asia, but have a strict budget in place. Malaysia already has a well-formed expat community — with a lot of Americans choosing to retire in Penang.

Other popular cities that Americans choose are Kuala Lumpur, Malacca, and Langkawi. Kuala Lumpur is the main hub in Malaysia — there's malls on every street corner, restaurants for every cuisine, and a mix of the suburbs and city. Penang is the most traditional of the bunch — it has a very typical Southeast Asia vibe, and massive bonus: it's also by the water! You can easily find a villa or apartment with a sea-view here, and there's a bunch of beaches all around.

Langkawi has a resort vibe to it and is located in the Andaman Sea. It's close to the Thai border. Langkawi is great for those looking for a total retirement getaway, and is a lot more remote and rural feeling than the other cities in Malaysia. Malacca is less popular than the other 3 cities for retirement purposes; however, a good amount of American retirees have found a happy home here. Malacca is located on the coast that divides Malaysia and Indonesia. It's a beautiful, tropical haven surrounded by water and good food.

If you think Malaysia is the right destination for your retirement then you can go ahead and easily apply for a retirement visa, as long as you can show that you have a monthly income/ retirement pension of about $2,500. Another popular country in Asia that Americans choose to retire is **Vietnam.**

Vietnam is an incredibly cheap place to live, which is why so many expats are flocking there! You can live a life of extreme luxury in Vietnam for around $2,500 USD a month. This includes rent in a premium location, food, utilities, transportation, and entertainment. Vietnam is filled with lush jungles, vibrant cities, idyllic farmlands that stretch throughout the country. The beauty and versatility of this country make it an easy place to fall in love with, and an even easier place to call home. It's also an incredibly safe place to live; with significantly lower crime rates than France, Greece, and the US.

The important thing to note here is that Vietnam does not offer a retirement visa; so, most people that have retired here have done so on a tourist visa. Tourist visas allow you to stay in the country for about 1 to 3 months, but are renewable for a small fee. Americans that retire here leave the country every 3 months for a short trip, before returning back to Vietnam.

Vietnam is a hub in Southeast Asia and is an excellent base for travel so many retirees choose Vietnam for this exact reason! They use it as a chance to travel and explore Southeast Asia at a leisurely pace. Leaving every 3 months allows you to explore the rest of Southeast Asia, and when you return back to Vietnam your visa is valid for another 3 months. This cycle goes on and on. Sidenote: You can get a tourist visa for 5 years in Vietnam BUT only if your parents or spouse are Vietnamese citizens.

Since retiring here isn't as easy or straightforward as other countries, it's only a good option if you like the idea of traveling every couple months and visiting a new part of Southeast Asia. If traveling and moving around isn't the type of retirement you're looking for then Vietnam is definitely not for you.

Turning the globe away from Asia and looking instead at Europe leads us to **Spain**. Spain is one of the most popular options for American retirees who are looking at Europe. From great weather to affordable dining to a lively culture and entertainment scene, Spain truly has it all. History, art, architecture, music, and food are the cornerstones of Spain; of course, many expats move here to be close to the beach.

The Spanish coastline covers almost 5,000 kilometers and the sandy beaches are a hub for tanning, swimming, and water-sports.

Some of the most popular cities that expats choose to live in are Madrid, Barcelona, Costa Brava, Seville, and Orange Blossom Coast. Each city has its own particular merits and stories to tell. If you're looking for a busy, cosmopolitan city then Madrid and Barcelona are your best bets. If you're looking for beautiful landscapes, ocean views, sandy beaches, and traditional Spanish villages then you'd be happiest in Costa Brava or Orange Blossom Coast. Seville is definitely the best option for the romantics in the crowd, who are craving slow, gracious living with a dash of Southern Spanish charm.

No matter what city draws your attention, you need to apply for Spain's long-term residency card in order to live here. You should start the application process at home in the US, and once you receive the stamp in your passport you're free to travel to Spain and live there for a year. After the year is up, you can easily renew your residency for another 2 years. You can continue renewing your residency every 2 years until you apply for permanent residency. The main qualification for residency in Spain is that you show a minimum of 25,000 euros (roughly $30,000 USD) in a bank account in the country.

The last country on my list of popular retiree places is also in Europe. Of course, I'm talking about **France!** The most romantic of the romantics. Just the thought of France conjures up images of the Eiffel Tower, Louvre, Notre-Dame, French Riviera, and Versailles. Of course it's important to note that this "thought" does come with a hefty price tag. Retiring in France (specifically Paris) is one of, if not the, most expensive options. This is why I put it last on my list. While it is a popular place for American retirees and therefore worth mentioning, it's popular for a very particular group of people and certainly not the right choice for most of us!

While Paris is the dream for many and therefore comes with a price tag to match, there are more affordable options in France like the mountain town Annecy. The sparkling blue lake in the summer here is almost as beautiful as the snowy mountain peaks in the winter. If you're a fluent French speaker then another affordable option is Occitanie, a rural countryside in the south of France. This area has a bunch of affordable cities and towns sprinkled about, and has become increasingly popular with American retirees (specifically the French speaking ones)!

If drinking Champagne and Bordeaux in Paris is your dream, or you crave a seaside villa in Corsica, or all you want in retirement is to ski the Alpine slopes, then perhaps France is for you. In which case, you need to apply for France's long term residency card. You're qualified to apply for residency in France after you show proof of financial self-sufficiency and international medical insurance. After 3 years of living with this residency card, you're permitted to apply for a 10-year residency card.

Don't fret if France, or any other desirable places listed in this chapter, come at too high of a price tag. There are SO many more options I'm going to share with you. Options that are just as luxurious as sipping champagne at the Ritz, as adventurous as skiing in the Alps, as exciting as trekking the Inca Road, and just as fun as discovering pink river dolphins in Colombia. I have so many affordable and amazing options to run you through in my next chapter, so pour some wine, grab a pen, and start taking notes!

4. Wallet-Friendly Options Abroad

Remember: there is no such thing as the best place to live, the nicest place to be, or the coolest spot to retire. Just like most things in life, this isn't a one-size-fits-all type of situation. The most appealing thing about the world we live in are the limitless opportunities and places to be. If you love the idea of a certain place but can't afford to live there, then I guarantee you we can find find a similar place that fits into the mold you've always imagined.

So many of us want to follow our wanderlust instincts, but are scared that the fairy dust path they're leading us down will be too expensive and therefore not realistic. I'm here to tell you that's not the case at all! You can live a beautiful, exciting life abroad that is both dream-like and also wallet-friendly.

Living in Tokyo gave me an up-close look at how a modest lifestyle can feel rich. Tokyo is one of the most expensive cities in Asia and living there certainly comes with a price tag fitting for a Chanel bag, not Kate Spade. While living in Tokyo can be very expensive, a lot of the simple pleasures come at no cost, and if you spend money the right way then the fact of the matter is — Tokyo can absolutely be within your budget.

Known for its Harajuku fashion, Buddhist temples, skyscrapers that meet the clouds, and cherry blossom trees that color the streets below; Tokyo is every travelers dream. Living there taught me that most of the simple pleasures really are free! Therefore, you can learn to make any country (within reason) work for your budget. With that being said, there are a number of countries that are known purely for their affordable costs and easy living. So, if you are working with a tight budget then this list will be perfect for you.

To start out with, there's the obvious choice of **Thailand**. Thailand is one of the most popular options in Asia and many Americans choose to settle down here, primarily due to the VERY low cost of living. Of course, the warm weather and beautiful beaches are a lovely bonus! Thailand is a cultural hub that's rich in gilded palaces and

Buddhist temples. The beaches here run for miles and the country is known for its good food and premium relaxation. For all these reasons and more Thailand is a massive hotspot for foreigners. Their only requirements for retiree visas are that you have a set income (typically around $25,000 in your bank account) and that you are over 50 years of age.

There are a number of VERY affordable cities in Thailand that you can easily settle down in. To start out with, there's the laid-back city of **Chiang Mai**. There's already an established American retiree base here, filled with expats who have chosen to embrace an exotic wallet-friendly lifestyle. Couples can comfortably live under $1,500 USD a month here. This includes rent, utilities, food, transportation, and entertainment. Most locals and expats that live here travel around on bike, eat noodle at local stands for most meals, and spend their weekends at the night market or tanning on the beaches.

Speaking of beaches, when it comes to the ideal beach lifestyle it doesn't get better than **Koh Samui**. Turquoise ocean contrasted with white-sand beaches and fragmented limestone cliffs, this spot is the pinnacle of relaxation, and is still rooted in the typical Thai culture you would hope for. Expats compare the laid-back, tropical lifestyle here to that of Hawaii, but FAR cheaper. Just like Chiang Mai, living in Koh Samui averages to about $1,500 USD a month for couples. Night markets offer supremely delicious local food for $2! These markets are sprinkled throughout the city (and pretty much all of Thailand) and they're a favorite for both locals and foreigners alike.

There's also a bunch of activities you can find in both Chiang Mai and Koh Samui that are affordable and fun. From exploring temples and Buddhist statues to water sports to jungle trekking, there's truly something for everyone. Similarly there's also something for everyone in Ecuador! **Ecuador** is one of the most affordable places to live in Latin America. A country filled with culture and with fun — just like Thailand!

Much like Thailand, Ecuador too is filled with beauty, culture, and fun activities — you can trek The Inca Road, surf in the Galapagos Islands, mountain bike through the Cotopaxi Volcano, and explore the Amazon Jungle. There's also a rich culture weaved throughout Ecuador and this is made clear by the local festivals, food, and historic city centers.

I already talked about Ecuador in my last chapter, as it's not only an affordable place to live but also a very popular place to live. To retire here you simply need to show a monthly income/retirement pension of $800 USD or more. Many Americans choose Ecuador for the cultural immersion, others choose it for its fun and beauty, but most choose it for its VERY low cost of living. A couple can comfortably live in Ecuador for about $1,500 — $2,000 USD a month. This includes rent, utilities, food, transportation, and entertainment.

Cuenca is one of the largest cities in Ecuador, it's also one of the most affordable, AND one of the most popular hubs for expats. This city is known for its buzzing expat culture, vibrant festivals, delicious local cuisines, and gorgeous scenery. Cuenca is also a very pedestrian-friendly city;

in fact, most locals and expats choose not to own a car and instead get around easily via taxis, buses, or even just walking. The city is so beautiful and easy to get around by foot so you really want to capitalize on this. Not only are you getting in some great exercise, but you're also exploring and taking in some great scenery.

The streets are coated in cobblestone, sidewalks are created with walkers and cyclers in mind — it's truly a wonderful experience just getting from point A to point B! And of course, if you're looking for specific areas to explore and meander through, a great place to start are the art galleries. Cuenca is the artistic mecca of southern Ecuador. You'll find the most amazing and unique ceramics, jewelry, custom-made instruments, and leather goods in this city. Even if you're not looking to buy, window-shopping is just as fun!

Of course, if you're talking about fun, cheap, and popular you have to talk about **Mexico**! As mentioned in my previous chapter, Mexico is a very popular destination for American retirees — it just so happens to be a very affordable destination as well. There's a bunch of different options here, from small villages to big cities. Not to mention, Mexico already has a developed expat community so assimilating and fitting in here is a very simple task.

To apply for a temporary resident visa in Mexico, you need to qualify under one of the following criteria:

1.) Can show a monthly income/ retirement pension of about $1,400

2.) Own property in Mexico with a value of $210,000 or more

If you're thinking of retiring in Mexico then one of the most affordable cities here is **Mazatlán**. An expat-favorite, this city is perfect for the wallet-crunchers! It has the ultimate trio — good weather, good prices, and absolutely gorgeous scenery. There's miles of sandy beaches, delicious fresh seafood, friendly locals, and a vibrant cultural scene. You can comfortably live here for under $1,200 USD — this includes rent, utilities, groceries, transportation, and entertainment.

Mazatlán offers an exciting array of entertainment and events, as it has a strong cultural scene woven into the city. The Plaza Machado is a well-renowned music and dance school that lights up the city, the Angela Peralta Theater is home to beautiful pieces of dance and theater, and the oceanfront malecon is home to international runners and cyclists. This city is a true cultural hub and will keep you both entertained and relaxed throughout your time here. Activities range from visits to the local farmers market to festivals on the beach to comedy clubs. No matter your preference, you will find some real treasures in Mazatlán.

As you can see, the two cornerstones of Mexico are beautiful beaches and a vibrant culture. Both these cornerstones hold strong in Nicaragua as well. This is my final suggestion for a wallet-friendly retirement. **Nicaragua** has a very low cost of living for a very high quality of life! Simply put, most couples can comfortably and happily live here for about $1,500 USD a month. This includes rent, utilities, transportation, food, and entertainment.

Nicaragua has a retiree program similar to Costa Rica's. In order to live here, you must first gain residency, then you can get a retirement visa. To gain residency in Nicaragua the main requirement is that you show that you have a monthly income/ retirement pension of about $600 USD. This is obviously a much lower amount than other countries require, which is a huge bonus for the wallet-crunchers in the audience! If you're strongly considering Nicaragua as a viable option then your best bet would be to retire in the city of León.

León is one of the most affordable, expat-friendly cities in Nicaragua. This city is designed for walking so owning a car here is certainly not a necessity. León, much like the rest of Nicaragua, offers a wide range of activities. These activities include sailing at sunset, watching ballet shows, deep-sea fishing, volcano boarding, hiking, and exploring the numerous churches and art museums at you disposal. León is also one of the oldest cities in Central America and life here is as simple, slow, and relaxed as it was when the city was first founded in 1524!

Depending on your preference, you may be looking for a slow-paced life like the one in León, or if the pull is strong perhaps you're looking for excitement and adventure. Some people may crave a small cottage in a fishing village while others opt for a large condo in a bustling city. You may love the ocean and the salty air that it comes with or you may hate the humidity, and opt instead for chilly days in the mountains.

My point is — we all have different visions of what our ideal retirement looks like and while I've highlighted some of the most affordable cities in this chapter, perhaps money is of no concern and you simply want the best there is to offer. You want champagne at sunset, a villa on the ocean, and a view as clear and tranquil as your mind on a lazy Sunday. You want Prada bags, 5-star restaurants, a maid, a driver, and a large house filled with the best that money can buy. If this is what you're looking for then my next chapter was tailor-made for you!

5. Living the Luxury Life: Prime Destinations

Some of us work our whole lives under the constraints of making enough money for our families, worrying about making a name for ourselves, worrying about leaving behind a legacy, constantly thinking about work even in our free-time and on weekends.

These types of constraints take a toll on our minds and our bodies; so, when we finally leave our work behind we feel sadness of course, but above all — relief. Relief for a second chapter, relief for a new phase, relief for our next adventure, and relief that we can finally have some rest and relaxation.

This relaxation can present itself in a variety of different ways: a beachside villa, a haven in the mountains, a cottage in a quaint Spanish village, and if your money allows — a life of extreme luxury in a prime destination.

If you're looking for the ultimate retirement and money isn't your primary concern then this chapter is for you.

When most of us picture a life of luxury, we curate a vision in our minds of island-life, mojitos on the beach, beautiful sunsets, and villas on the tip of a cliff overlooking water. This image comes to life in **Bermuda**. Bermuda is known for its beautiful pink sandy beaches that serve as a stark contract to the turquoise waters; a perfect destination for swimming, snorkeling, exploring reefs and shipwrecks. The warm, palmy subtropical weather is also ideal for tanning, relaxing, and just overall lazing. The beaches on this island are one of the many draws, Bermuda also has gorgeous architecture, pastel houses, and a rich culture that has formed through Caribbean, Portuguese, African, and British influences.

Leisure and luxury are at the forefront of this island. A mix of old-world glam, boutique hotels, cultural immersion, pristine blue waters, and large golf course. This island was created as the perfect retirement destination and in order to live here, you need to own property — either in the form of a vacation home or a permanent home! Many of the houses here are fit for kings and queens and look as though they've escaped out of movie sets and fairytale fantasies.

Bermuda has a variety of mansions on top of hills, set against the turquoise ocean, overlooking golf courses. There's also mansions with infinity pools, spas, tennis courts, oceanfront dining, and massive outdoor gardens. Additionally, Bermuda has quaint colorful houses dotted along the hills, and pastel cottages located close to the pink beaches. No matter what your affinity or your pref-erence is, I can tell you — without a shadow of a doubt — Bermuda has it all. It's the ultimate destination for a life of luxe and lush.

The cost for a luxurious life in Bermuda will depend on where you live, whether you rent or buy, how much you're willing to spend on outdoor dining and entertainment, and a multitude of other factors. Bermuda is one of the most expensive places to live, but it is also one of the most luxurious and opulent. Bermuda offers a number of ac-tivities and attractions. You can spend a day tanning and swimming at Horseshoe Bay Beach. You can hike along the South Shore Trail. You can spend the day snorkeling, scuba diving, and exploring colorful coral reefs. You can indulge in glass-bottom boat tours, botanical gardens, art galleries, and museums. I told you, Bermuda really does have it all!

Speaking of having it all, the next country on my list is **Switzerland**. My memories of Switzerland are some of my favorite memories of all time. I visited about 7 years ago and to this day, I remember everything about it. I vividly remember the tour we took of the Lindt Chocolate factory — never have I tasted so much chocolate, not only that — but the chocolate was so creamy and delicious! I also remember the lush greenery that ran throughout Switzerland — I remember fields of open green and sheep gently grazing along the meadows. I remember the kind people, the cool crisp weather, and the aquamarine water.

Switzerland is one of the most luxurious places in the world, and while any city here would satisfy your cozy retirement itch, my recommendation is Zurich. Not only does Zurich have an already established expat community but it also happens to be one of the most beautiful cities in the world. Zurich is the largest city in Switzerland and given how large it is, there›s a multitude of attractions and activities available for locals and expats alike.

When people conjure up an image of Zurich they think of delicious chocolates, luxury shopping, and unrelenting beauty. What many don't think about is the number of attractions and activities that Zurich has to offer. Zurich is known for its amazing museums, world-renowned architecture, and luxurious art galleries. On the flip side of this, Zurich also has several hiking trails, lakes to swim in, and zoos to tour. The perfect destination for singles, families, and retirees!

Zurich's Old Town is one of the most beautiful places, and it has great rentals and houses to buy. Old Town also houses some of Zurich's most famous museums; such as the Museum of Art and the Swiss National Museum. This area of the city is lined with cobblestones that lead you through tall colorful buildings, beautiful museums, and quirky restaurants.

7 years later and I don't think I'll ever forget Lake Zurich. This beautiful lake is shaped like a banana and is a popular spot for tourists and expats alike. Many people venture out here for peace and relaxation. Some choose to run along the water, while others enjoy boat trips through the lake.

At the eastern tip of Lake Zurich you'll find Rapperswil Rose Gardens, commonly referred to as Rose Town. This gorgeous garden is filled with almost 20,000 rose bushes in full bloom! Also, the world-famous Lindt Chocolate Factory is not too far from here either and you NEED to check that out! Trust me! If chocolate and gorgeous lakes don't entice you then perhaps you'll be interested to know that Zurich also has amazing museums, art galleries, and zoos. The city life and abundance of activities here are balanced with beauty and opulence.

Living in Zurich is as posh and luxurious as it gets and the price tag will definitely attest to that! The cost for a luxurious life in Zurich, and anywhere else in Switzerland, will depend on where you live, whether you rent or buy, how much you're willing to spend on outdoor dining and entertainment, and a multitude of other factors.

To live in Zurich or anywhere else in Switzerland you'll need to apply for a D visa (longterm residency). You can apply for this as long as you tick the following boxes:

• You're not seeking employment in Switzerland

• You have both accident coverage and health insurance from an approved provider

• You have the financial means to support yourself

• You have a close connection to Switzerland (property here, family member here, or have visited multiple times before)

If you tick all these boxes then you can consider a life in Switzerland. However, if Switzerland is not for you then you can look at something entirely different — like **Italy**.

If you're looking for the stereotypical Old World lifestyle then Italy is worthy of your attention. The old towns are quaint, the countryside is beautiful, and the cities are seething with culture, beauty, and luxury! There are so many Italian cities that could grant you a life of luxury, but one of the absolute best is Rome. Rome is the obvious choice for luxury and exclusivity. It's the largest city in Italy, it's also the city with the most famous and colorful history in the world.

The most expensive and luxurious area codes here would be Via Condotti, Via del Babuino, and Piazza di Spagna. These areas are filled with historic homes and buildings that showcase ornate ceilings, marble statues, and views of the rooftops of Rome. The city of Rome has a sort of immortal elegance to it that is defined by its charm, history, and grace.

Rome is a city of layered depth and as you peel back each layer you unearth more and more intrigue and beauty. This city has some of the most celebrated and prominent landmarks in all of Europe; such as the Pantheon, the Roman Forum, the Column of Marcus Aurelius, the Colosseum, Sistine Chapel, and Trevi Fountain. In addition to these relics of beauty, just walking down the cobbled streets and admiring the purple-pink-yellow-orange sunsets is a wonder of its own!

Rome is perfect for history-lovers who are looking to settle down somewhere that is posh and luxurious, but also rooted in culture and in history. The cost for a luxurious life in Rome, and anywhere else in Italy, will depend on where you live, whether you rent or buy, how much you're willing to spend on outdoor dining and entertainment, and a multitude of other factors.

If pizza, pasta, wine, and history are not what you're looking for then perhaps you'd be more interested in the island-city life of **Singapore**. Having grown up here and being a Singaporean citizen, I can't say enough good things about this country. But the one disclaimer I'll put at the very start of this blurb is that Singapore is expensive, even more expensive than the previous countries listed in this chapter.

Singapore is the second most expensive country in Asia, following closely in Hong Kong's footsteps. It's also in the top 5 most expensive places to retire in the world. It's expense is tied with its exclusivity, its luxury, and its prime EVERYTHING — from its food to its malls to its beaches and nightclubs, Singapore is the very definition of luxe and luxury.

I loved my time in Singapore. I loved living in a country where the beach was as close to you as the mall was. A country that was as rich in culture as it was in money. A country where the food court at the mall was as gourmet as any 5-star restaurant. I fell in love with the culture, the colors, the smells, and the vibrant nature that made this country what it was.

Most people I know had a very similar experience with Singapore — whether they hailed from the UK or the US, Europe or other parts of Asia — they all fell in love with Singapore and were easily able to make it their home.

Singapore is a melting pot of cultures and this diversity gives the country a very special and unique feel. Ideas flourish here and grow, progress is part of the country's fabric, cultural diversity is of prime importance, and the cuisines, styles, and languages of the country reflect that of the world. Culturally, Singapore is very similar to the US but it also has a flair and touch of other influences. You can find world-famous chili crab and laksa here, but you can also find the best tacos, sandwich delis, pizza parlors, and chicken tikka masala!

The food is just one representation of Singapore's cultural diversity, you see it all over — in their literature, their art, their fashion, and in the faces walking the streets. While many expats move here for this "melting pot" styled culture, others move here for the luxury lifestyle, beautiful sites, and the fun activities. From biking along the water at East Coast Park to swimming at the infinity pool miles high in Marina Bay Sands, Singapore offers a number of gems.

Locals and expats love having cheap beers and midnight feasts at the Hawker Centers. These outdoor food courts house a number of ethnic and local dishes. The flavors represent the flavors of the world from Chinese, Malay, Indian to Western. Another massive draw in Singapore are the Gardens by the Bay — a beautifully designed green space filled with flourishing plant life; this is the perfect escape from city-life. The Supertree Grove here has a cluster of iconic structures and the Cloud Forest Dome has the world's tallest indoor waterfall! The biodiversity at Gardens by the Bay is beautiful and frankly, quite astounding.

Orchard Road on the other hand is a complete representation of Singapore's bustling city life. Lined with beautiful malls and high-end stores, Orchard Road is a shoppers paradise. This neighborhood boasts 22 malls and 6 department stores, as well as 4 movie theaters, and a number of karaoke establishments, restaurants, and arcades. Living on or near Orchard Road can get very expensive as this area is super lucrative.

One of the best things about Singapore is its mix of city and tropics. If you drive about 40 minutes from Orchard Road you›ll arrive at Sentosa Island, another popular area where expats and retirees buy and rent homes. Siloso Beach is one of the beaches here and it›s perfect if you're looking to swim, tan, or just relax by the water. There's also an underwater aquarium where you can swim with dolphins and the famous Merlion statue, which showcases the head of a lion and the body of a fish.

There are a number of water parks and amusement parks all throughout Singapore — such as Universal Studios, Adventure Cove Waterpark, Wave House Sentosa, and River Safari. The River Safari is amazing, as is the Night Safari. I can't even tell you the number of times I've been to the night safari in Singapore! As soon as you enter there's a heart-thumping fire show where performers put on a display of fire-twirling and flame-throwing stunts.

Then as you enter the safari, you're privy to a number of different shows showcasing the creatures of the night, and of course this leads to the main event — where you take a tram ride through the safari. You can get off the tram at any point to walk through one of the trails; such as the bat cave trail, leopard trail, and fishing cat trail. You'll see pretty much every animal on this safari, from the Asian Elephants to the Clouded Leopards to the Malayan Tigers. Seeing these animals at nighttime certainly adds a layer of mystique and excitement!

Singapore has so many exciting activities like these, and there's also so many elements of pamper and luxe. From spice gardens, to rooftop bars that showcase the entire city, to the most exclusive neighborhoods, to 5-star restaurants and hotels, Singapore is the queen of luxury. Most people here are millionaires, and plenty are billionaires; so, the lifestyle is definitely a representation of that wealth. The vast majority of locals and expats have full-time maids, drivers, and cooks. Think of the movie "Crazy, Rich Asians" but maybe dial it back a bit! The country is truly filled with culture, color, money, and luxury.

The cost for a luxurious life in Singapore will depend on where you live, whether you rent or buy, how much you're willing to spend on outdoor dining and entertainment, and a multitude of other factors. In order to live in Singapore you'll need to apply for permanent residency — the most common route for permanent residency is through an employment pass or by being the spouse of a Singaporean citizen.

If you don't tick either of those boxes then you can look into becoming a foreign investor in Singapore through the Global Investor Program. This program will grant you permanent residency in Singapore. To qualify for this, you must invest at least S$2.5 million in a new business startup, expansion of an existing business operation, or a GIP-approved fund that invests in Singapore-based companies.

Of course, this route isn't for everyone, and Singapore can certainly feel a little too expensive, extravagant, and strict for some. If the countries listed in this chapter aren't for you, then don't fret — we still have so much more to cover!

If luxury and opulence aren't the prime focus for your retirement plans, and you'd prefer a house deep in the mountains or a bungalow by the beach then keep on reading — my next chapter will guide you down the perfect path.

6. Best Beach Options & Mountain Options

The vast majority of people have their heart set on a new life at the beach or in the mountains. If that's something you deem to be important in retirement then you need a clear agenda on how you'll get there and where exactly "there" is. This chapter will first highlight the best beach options to consider — spots that showcase world-class sun, sand, sea, and surf. The second part of this chapter will focus on the best escapes to the mountains, where the weather's cool and brisk and the views are breathtaking.

If you're looking to live so close to the ocean that you taste the salt in the air then you can't go wrong with hidden gem #1 — **Mauritius**! Mauritius has an unbelievably diversified cultural mix of the Indian Ocean; it brings together a variety of exotic traditions, cultures, and foods.

This "melting pot" lifestyle has attracted a numbers of ex-pats and retirees.

Mauritius has the most beautiful tropical beaches, but it also has quality health care and a booming environment — making it an easy transition for retirees. Something else that makes it an easy transition? The surreal beauty of this country. Never before would you have seen bluer water, whiter sand, and sunnier skies!

The North of Mauritius has the most beautiful beaches, like Péreybère, Mont-Choisy, and Grand-Bay. These heav-enly beaches invite utter relaxation in the shade of Bel Ombre trees. This area is also teeming with water-sports and street-food trucks. Right next to the red-roofed No-tre-Dame Auxiliatrice Church, you'll see fishermen at the end of the day selling their best catch to the resi-dents, who have arrived with open baskets and hungry stomachs! The overall atmosphere and vibe here is very friendly and laid-back; it's exactly what you'd expect of island-life.

If you travel a little West you'll arrive at the capitol of the country, Port Louis. This beautiful, vibrant city is teeming with life — from the historic churches to the museums and colorful markets, this city is a true gem. It's a perfect place to settle down in retirement — as it not only pro-vides you with the ultimate beach vibes, but also amazing city vibes! The palm trees face the harbor, the aromatic smells of fruit cloud the markets, and the people wear smiles so big that you feel right at home.

A life in Mauritius, as a couple, will cost roughly $1,200 — $1,600 USD. This includes rent, utilities, food, entertainment, and transportation. This pricing is accurate for all cities here — including Port Louis; but also QuatreBornes, Curepipe, Beau Bassin-Rose Hill, and Moka. It's important to note that all these cities have an existing expat presence, so you'll fit in easily.

The cities in Mauritius have beautiful architecture, inspired in part by their colonial history. Therefore the Dutch, British, and French influences are all subtly visible in Mauritius's architectural designs. The food is influenced by this Colonial history as well; making the cuisine in Mauritius both diverse and delicious! The beaches are all beautiful and while most are public, some belong to luxury gated communities — in case that's something you're interested in.

Cruising away from Mauritius, my next pick for the ideal beach retirement would have to be The **Dominican Republic.**

The Dominican Republic is famous for its world-class beautiful beaches, that attract massive volumes of tourists every year. These powdery coasts, however, are not only the ideal vacation spot, but also an ideal retirement spot! There's so much more to the Dominican Republic than its famous beaches.

This country is fairly small, yet it offers around a thousand miles of immaculate white-sand beaches, with only a few people sprinkled about. Tourists are primarily gathered in the resort area, so most of the beaches are people-free zones! The country also has a special visa that caters to American retirees so moving here is a breeze. The only qualification you need to meet is that you must show a minimum monthly income/ retirement pension of $1,500.

Once this qualification is met and your visa has been processed, you're free to live anywhere in the Dominican Republic. One of the best coastal spots to settle down here is Las Terrenas. The town has a great mix of the tropical Caribbean life as well as the cosmopolitan city life. It's the type of town where your craving for French baguettes, farm-fresh gnocchi, and Cotija cheese can easily be catered to at any point during the day! The French and Italian influences here are prominent, as the Italians and French settled down in this town ages ago and have since created diverse culinary and infrastructure businesses that cater to their fellow expats.

The town itself is a perfect beach haven, offering miles of inshore waters and white-sand beaches. The town is sprinkled with beautiful palm trees and pastel-colored fishing boats. Giving it a true island feel! The slow gusts of wind and the warm temperature give this island a year-round balmy and tropical feel. Another popular option for expats is Punta Cana. One of the most popular towns in the Dominican Republic, Punta Cana has some of the best infrastructure and beaches in the country. The town is packed with shops, restaurants, malls, and bars. If you're looking for a sheer escape from the hustle and bustle of city life, then escaping to this beach-town is the perfect retirement option for you.

You can start your day at the picturesque Macao Beach, where you soak up the sun and waves, and you can end your day inside a cave nightclub or an exclusive restaurant. There's also so many sites and activities here to enjoy, so if you're looking for a more active and fun retirement then this is the ideal spot for you. You can take a zip-lining course, explore history at Altos de Chavon, sail to Isla Saona, or golf along the oceanside at Corales Golf Course.

However, if the Caribbean lifestyle isn't quite what you're looking for then perhaps you'd be happier in **Panama**.

I discussed Panama in some detail in chapter 3. For a quick recap: Panama has a low cost of living; so much so, that American retirees can live here peacefully and luxuriously while spending less than $3,000 USD a month. This includes utilities, rent, groceries, and even entertainment. Panama is also fairly close to the US making it easy to fly home for the holidays or even just for nostalgia trips. There's also an incredibly affordable health care system here; as well as, a reliable metro-system, amazing infrastructure, and well-paved roads. All this paired with spectacular ocean views and warm weather, make Panama the perfect destination for American retirees who are looking for a beach getaway!

Also, as I discussed early on, Panama has something called the pensionada program (commonly referred to as the "retired visa program"). As an American retiree, you qualify for this program by having a pension of at least $1,000 USD a month. Once you're approved to be a part of this program, you can live in Panama for as long as you please!

The beaches here are gorgeous and one of the best beach-cities you can live in is Las Tablas. The city boasts some of the most beautiful beaches in the world, which is why dozens of Canadian and American retirees have settled down here. In addition to the luxurious beaches, Las Tablas also has a very authentic cultural presence. This is made apparent by their customs, traditions, folk-lore, and festivals. The Pollera Festival for example takes places in July and hundreds of local women wear ornate handmade dresses and dance on the streets to festive and traditional Panamanian music! This festival centers around dance, music, street food, drinking, and fireworks.

Switching gears a bit here and traveling away from white-sand beaches to the pinnacles of tall mountains! My favorite destination for an escape to the mountains is Croatia.

Life moves at a super slow and relaxed pace in **Croatia**; sailboats peacefully drift along the shimmering Adriatic Sea, palm trees line the promenade, and rosemary and lavender aromas flow through the air.

Croatia has over a thousand islands and only a few dozen are inhabited! While most people associate Croatia as a beach destination (and this is certainly true) there's a few hidden gems here that serve as the perfect retirement in the mountains! One such region is called Istria. This triangle-shaped peninsula runs along the coast of Italy and is a beautiful region of Croatia filled with meadows, olive groves, and even vineyards.

The rolling hills and mountains here are spotted with white-stone villages that can be traced back to the Middle Ages.

Istria is a true hidden gem, located in Croatia but heavily influenced by all things Italian. The mountainside is a beautiful place to live, and the region itself is the perfect mix of mountain and city. Living in the mountains has its perks — solace, privacy, peace, and beauty. But when you have that amazing mix of mountain-life and cosmopolitan-life, like you do here, it truly is the perfect combination.

Istria is well-known for the fabulous festivals held here! From the New Wine Festival (recognizing the best wine-makers) to the Truffle Festival (where dozens of truffle hunters search for black and white truffles in the region) to the annual summer film festival, Istria is crawling with culture!

Another great option for mountain-living with a cultural immersion is **Ecuador**. I discussed Ecuador in great detail in chapter 4, as it is one of the most affordable places to live in Latin America.

> **Ecuador is a country filled with culture and fun, and is the ideal destination for a mountain escape.**

Similar to Croatia, Ecuador too is filled with beauty, culture, and is a very affordable place to live. As previously discussed, to retire in Ecuador you simply need to show a monthly income/retirement pension of $800 USD or more. Additionally, a couple can comfortably live in Ecuador for about $1,500 — $2,000 USD. This includes rent, utilities, food, transportation, and entertainment for the month.

Combine this low cost of living with the unparalleled beauty of Ecuador and you have an undeniably perfect combination! If you're looking for an escape to the mountain you can't go wrong with Cuenca. As discussed in chapter 4, Cuenca is one of the largest cities in Ecuador, it's also one of the most popular hubs for expats, and the perfect destination for a retirement in the mountains.

Cuenca lies in an intermontane basin of the Andes Mountains, on the Matadero River. If mountain-living is your goal then you truly can't go wrong with Cuenca. Living here feels like an actual dream! The streets are lined with cobblestone, the art galleries are inspiring, and the views are spectacular.

The climate in Cuenca is also spectacular — it's pretty much springtime year-round! In fact, most locals and expats leave their windows open throughout the day to let in the crisp mountain air. While there are some cheaper cities in Ecuador for retirement purposes, the balance between lifestyle and a low cost of living is the best in Cuenca.

Cuenca also boasts very impressive modern infrastructure and architecture. Many of the buildings here are UNESCO-protected, so you know that the city will hold on to its colonial feel for for years to come. The culture in Cuenca, much like the rest of Ecuador, is in full display via art galleries, the orchestra, music shows and live dancing. Even the food is a work of art here! There are endless options for fine dining, as well as endless options for cafés that offer traditional food at superb prices.

Cuenca often feels like a city from another age. The mountain views, cobbled streets, and colonial architecture all provide Cuenca with an aura of peace and tranquility that's difficult to find elsewhere.

7. No Language or Cultural Barriers

Sometimes the easiest course of action is all we're looking for. A true home away from home, where we can live in the tropics or the mountains but feel like we haven't traveled too far away. Familiar surroundings put us at ease and make us feel at home.

Eating the same types of foods, hearing the same languages we've heard all our lives, having similar road names and grocery products. These types of similarities make it easier to adjust to a foreign country. If you're looking for comfort but still want charm then you'd be happiest in countries that are most similar to the US and have minimal cultural barriers, as well as zero language barriers.

Moving from Singapore to the US had zero cultural implications for me; both countries were so similar that when I moved here 9 years ago, I felt as though I had never left Singapore. Both countries are proficient in English, have a deeply western background, have similar currencies, similar values, even look, sound, and smell the same! Therefore there was no adjustment period and I was immediately able to adapt and blend in. To this day, people are shocked to hear that I grew up in Singapore and not in the US — that's how aligned the two countries are.

There are so many benefits to this type of move. With the biggest benefit being the ease at which you acclimate into society. There's also a comfort in the familiar and you find solace in seeing things you've seen your whole life. There are a number of countries, besides Singapore, that have a similar cultural background to the US. The first one that springs to mind is **Ireland**.

Ireland runs on English, with only a handful of people (less than 6%) speaking Irish Gaelic. Of course, the thick Irish accent makes our mundane English language sound far more elusive and exotic! Ireland is unbelievably similar to the US, not only do they speak the same language here; but the culture, values, and food are all closely aligned to what we're used to. This offshore island is located in the North Atlantic, and has been strongly influenced by Western culture since its genesis.

Also, the architecture in Ireland is almost the exact same as the architecture here in the US, with both countries having similarly styles, similar government buildings, similar stores, restaurants, and houses. The social customs are also strikingly similar, as are the sports and leisure activities. Both countries share a love of golf, horse-racing, and football. Even the stores in Ireland replicate the ones back home — from a surplus of Disney stores to Tommy Hilfiger to Swarovski and Pandora, Ireland is filled with American stores, boutiques, and fashion brands.

While the culture here is predominantly Western oriented, there are bits of indigenous culture thrown in through the presence of Irish music and Gaelic games. Famous for their love of food, drink, and dance, the Irish also have booming cities and a picturesque countryside. Everything here is beautiful. Additionally, it's a great place to live. Ireland has a prime location as it is one of the closest European countries to both Canada and the US so you can easily fly home at the drop of a hat. You also have all of Europe at your fingertips so you can travel and explore as much as you'd like. The UK is about an hour away, Rome is barely 3 hours away, and Barcelona is a mere 2 hour flight!

Fly about 20 hours from Ireland and you'll land in **Australia**! Another great country to settle down in if you're looking for a similar cultural environment to the US. Australia is one of the most beautiful countries I've ever visited and what struck me most was how similar the culture, vibe, and atmosphere was to the US. The primary language there is English and the people are extroverted and friendly, similar to the people here.

I remember being struck by Australia's beauty — the golden sand on the beaches, the great oceans, the lush greenery, and open landscape. It was all so warm and welcoming! We spent most of our time there in Sydney — roaming Sydney Harbor, swimming at Bondi beach, exploring Chowder Bay and Bare Island. Everywhere we went, we were astounded by the beauty and biodiversity. Bare Island sported a number of soft corals and sea stars, as well as pygmy pipe fish, and pygmy seahorses. Chowder Bay on the other hand had octopus, blennies, squid, decorator crabs, and frog fish.

As amazing as the biodiversity was, what we were most struck by was the food in Australia. Western fusion with a twist, that's how I would best describe it! Living in Australia you'd be able to find all the same foods you'd find back home, plus more. There's so many special gems all over Australia and one of our favorites was an area in South East Queensland called The Rainforest Way. We literally felt like we ate the rainbow here! From the jewel green limes to the sizzling pink dragon fruit to the golden mango and deep red cherries, the fruits we ate along this trail were the best I've ever had. They also happened to represent pretty much every color of the rainbow!

North of here, in Darwin, we ate the absolute best Laksa, a spicy noodle soup that's a local favorite. We also found places with beer on tap and amazing burgers, pasta joints that would make Little Italy jealous, delicious chicken tenders and fries, and pho right from the kitchen of a Vietnamese family. The foods of Australia aren't the only thing that resemble Western culture, the language, atmosphere, values, all align with the US. This is definitely a place you'd feel right at home!

However, if you're looking to feel at home but with the addition of tropical weather and tranquil waters, then your best bet would be **Belize**.

An English-speaking country, Belize packs a whole bunch of charm, tranquility, and scenery into one tiny place! The laidback, peaceful, Caribbean lifestyle here is a massive draw for retirees, especially considering there's no language barrier and the culture aligns quite well with the US. The culture here is so easy to adjust to, and there's also a number of fun activities and unique landscapes to explore.

Ambergris Caye is the largest island in Belize and is also one of the most popular places that locals and expats choose to settle down in. In fact there's already an established community of American and Canadian expats and retirees living here.

The downtown scene in Ambergris Caye is fun, lively, and is teeming with beach bars and restaurants. Snorkeling, diving, and swimming are huge here and basically a lifestyle choice; so this is definitely the ideal retirement spot for you if you're looking for a tropical retirement with remnants and the ease of home.

If you like the idea of an island-life but prefer a smaller, more quaint location, then Hopkins is a great match for you. Hopkins is the smallest fishing village in Belize and has retained most of its seaside charm. The friendly people here will remind you of being back home. The culture all over Belize is friendly, welcoming, and familiar so you don't have to worry about culture shock here at all. With English being the dominant language here, you'll also have an easy time acclimating and getting around.

Some of the most beautiful and well-known sites and attractions in Belize include The Great Blue Hole — an ocean sinkhole ideal for divers; Belize Barrier Reef,

Caracol Natural Monument — ruins of a sprawling Mayan city, and the Belize Zoo. Retiring here would ensure not only an easy transition, but also a tropical paradise filled with beautiful sites and fun activities!

I'm going to close this chapter with what I assume is the most obvious choice for a retirement that is close to home, similar to home, with zero cultural or language barriers. I'm talking of course about **Canada**! Canada is by far the most similar country to the US — with zero cultural or language barriers. So if you're looking to fly the nest but not fly very far, then Canada is the perfect option for you.

There is a massive community of American retirees and expats living in various cities across Canada so you'll have no issues acclimating. Culturally, the environment here is the same as the US so there will be no adjustment period. You'll also be so close to home so you can fly back as much as you want, and depending on where you settle down in Canada — you could even drive home!

From lakes and mountains to urban life, Canada is known for its lush greenery and beautiful nature. The waters here are also teeming with wildlife — from sea otters to orcas, you'll find it all. Canada is a culturally easy environment, but it also provides a beautiful and relaxed setting for your retirement.

There are so many amazing attractions and sites that deserve your attention here; such as Big Muddy Badlands in Saskatchewan, Red Sands at Prince Edward Island, Capilano Suspension Bridge Park in British Columbia, Cathedral Grove on Vancouver Island, and Lake Louise at Banff

National Park. The sites here are truly breathtaking, and well worth your time!

8. Budgeting your Life Overseas

This is the point in the book where I expect you to start getting excited! After perusing the various countries you can retire in, I'm sure you're starting to formulate a plan to move to one of these places. Maybe you're excited to explore the mountains in Ecuador or the beaches in Mauritius; or maybe a life of luxury in Switzerland is exactly what you need. So you know now where you want to go, the question is — how do you get there, from a logistics standpoint? How much money do you need to move to your desired country? How much money do you have to live on? These are the questions I'm going to address in this chapter.

Whether you're looking to retire in a wallet-friendly country (as described in chapter 4) or the most luxurious country in the world (as detailed in chapter 5), you need a blueprint for your new life overseas. Steps to follow when it comes to budgeting this new phase of your life.

If you're looking to grow your allotted money for your life abroad then one course of action would be to sell everything that you own. While this may sound harsh and scary, it's the perfect way to create cash flow for your life abroad. By liquidating all the assets you have, you would be left with a large amount of capital. Once you have this capital in your hand, the next step would be to invest this money.

Selling all your assets solves two things — 1. It creates cash flow for your new life and 2. It leaves you with less things to physically bring abroad. If you already have a well-established nest egg, then you may not need to take this approach. The important takeaway here is simply that you have some form of a **nest egg**. The amount that a "nest egg" qualifies is up to you and the type of life you're building.

As I've laid out in the chapters above, your nest egg can drastically change based on the country you choose and the lifestyle you're looking for.

Having a nest egg and having your finances in order is the first step to budgeting and creating a blueprint for your life overseas. Without this vital first step, you can't move on to the next steps of planning and formulating your new life. Once you have your nest egg together, the next step is to figure out how long the capital you've gathered will actually last. A great tool to help figure this out is an online calculator called FIRECalc (you can find this for free at **firecalc.com**).

This online calculator can help answer the most rudimentary question for planning your retirement: "Do I have enough money for the end of my life?" FIRECalc uses a database of bond and stock returns over the past century to figure out the answer to your question. You start by simply entering in how much money you have, how much longer you think you'll live (morbid, I know!), and how much you plan to spend per year. FIRECalc will then take into account increases due to inflation; and then, based on the answer you input into the calculator — you'll get a result that will let you know, IF, based on your current circumstances, your money will last through your retirement or if it will run out!

This online calculator is a super useful tool when figuring out if and where you can retire overseas. But it's only a useful tool if you've put together a nest egg. Of course, I understand that not everyone has a nest egg or a trust fund to rely on. If you don't have a nest egg or your nest egg simply isn't large enough to support a life overseas, then don't fret — there are other courses of action you can take.

Plainly put, if you don't have a nest egg to rely on then your only other feasible option is to **generate the income** that you need for your life overseas. It's important to remember that you probably will not be able to get a job in your desired country of residence since most places make it very difficult to acquire a work permit as foreign resident. But, what is possible, and honestly a lot easier, is to start your own business abroad!

As an expat, you have a huge advantage. Since you've come from a competitive, sophisticated, and advanced marketplace, you understand the concept of discovering a niche and filling it. A lot of the countries I've listed in the chapters above are far less developed and advanced than the US, so upon arrival you'll immediately notice areas that are lacking and can be filled in some sort of way. Capitalize on these ideas!

You'll definitely notice services that are frequently offered around the US but are not offered in your new country of residence. You can use these ideas to your advantage and implement them in some way or the other.

If becoming an entrepreneur and filling a gap in the countries economy is not something you want to do or something you feel you can manage, then the other option to create income is to earn money via a remote business. This could mean a number of things. The easiest idea would be to freelance for magazines or blogs (maybe even write about your experience in your new country). There are so many ways to earn additional income, depending on what your skillset and preferences are.

Once you've come up with a basic idea of how much money you have for your retirement, you can figure out what type of retirement your budget could buy you. It's important to remember that the majority of your budget will go into housing — in my next chapter (chapter 9), I will discuss in detail whether you should rent or buy a home based on your specific situation and finances. Your housing situation will drastically affect your cost of living. But again, this will be discussed in detail in the next chapter (chapter 9).

In addition to housing and property taxes (which will all be discussed in the next chapter), you also have to budget for **transportation**. Based on where you're planning to move, you need to figure out if you'll need a car or not. If you are planning to own a vehicle, then it's important to note that this will be your second biggest expense, after housing. If you're looking to escape to the mountains (as discussed in chapter 6) then you'll most likely need to invest in a car. But if you're planning to move to a big city where public transportation is easy to access then perhaps you won't need to invest in a vehicle.

It's also important to remember that the cost of the vehicle is only one part of your budget, the other part is cost of repairs for this vehicle. For example, if you are choosing to move to a remote mountain town then floods during the rainy season could lead to constant tire repairs and replacements. There's also the cost of gas to consider. If you would rather not deal with the cost and inconvenience of car ownership then you should definitely consider less remote options, and instead look at big cities that have good and easy public transportation.

You also need to budget for both **electricity** and **gas**. These utilities are important to factor in when creating your housing budget. In regards to electricity, if you're looking at places where you get all 4 seasons then you need to expect high electricity bills as chances are that you'll run the heat all through winter and the AC all through summer.

If you want to look at places where electricity won't be too high, then consider countries where the weather is spring-like year-round. This way you can get by with open windows and not use the heat or AC too much, if at all. Places like Panama, Colombia, and Ecuador have a number of cities where the weather is spring-like and cool year-round. In regards to gas, I'm of course referring to cooking gas. This will probably be your smallest expense but is still something to keep in mind when putting your budget together.

You also need to factor in **internet** and **phone** bills. If you're looking to get uninterrupted access to the internet 24/7 in a small town or somewhere in the mountains, then you need to expect hefty fees. In the bigger cities however you can get reliable, fast internet for a very reasonable price. In regards to your phone situation, all you really need to invest in overseas is a local cell phone and Zoom or Skype. In some cases you may want to purchase a landline as well. But again, this would be a smaller percentage of your budget so you don't have to worry too much about this one.

Television is something else to keep in mind when putting together your budget. Some people opt for cable TV as a way to stay connected to local culture and engage with the local community (via local talk shows and local news). However, most expats won't bother paying for cable and will instead just watch streaming services like Netflix, Amazon Prime, and Hulu.

While television won't be much of a high-ticket item, something you may want on the more extravagant side is household employees. A lot of American retirees choose to indulge in full-time help for the house. This is especially common in Asia, South America (pretty much any of the places I mentioned in chapter 4). A number of expats that settle down here will invest in household-help, that could come in the form of a full-time housekeeper, cook, or driver. Depending on your needs and your budget you could get 1 or even all 3. In some places getting a full-time, live-in housekeeper can be as cheap as $200 USD a month.

Of course, we can't create a reasonable budget without factoring in **food**. Groceries are going to be one of your primary expenses no matter where in the world you choose to live. Your food budget will also vary based on how often you choose to eat out and the places you choose to eat at. For example, if you're looking at food stalls or food courts versus restaurants then the cost could vary greatly. The more you get to know a place, you'll also be able to figure out the cheaper grocery stores and the more affordable restaurants to dine at.

Another variable that will drastically be impacted by where you live and how often you do it is **entertainment**. Much like your food budget, this is another expense that you have a lot of control over. Depending on how much you choose to eat out, go to the theatre, go for movies, and other outings, your entertainment budget could vary greatly. My biggest tip is to have a monthly budget and stick to it! It's very easy to get carried away with the allure of a new place and go over budget on entertainment, so having a set cost allocated to monthly entertainment is a great way to control yourself and mange your money.

If you're looking to keep entertainment costs low, you could always settle down in a place where there's little to spend money on. For example, if you settle down in a beach town, you could spend a lot of time just at the beach swimming, tanning etc. Another option is to choose a big city (like Tokyo or Paris) where there's a lot to do for free! From photo exhibits to walking at parks to exploring the city to gallery openings and museums, you can find a lot of free (or at least, very cheap) outings in big cities.

Much like entertainment, another big cost that you have a lot of control over is travel.

This includes trips back home as well as travel within your new country of residence. Depending on how often you plan to return home, you'll need to set aside some money for this. You'll also need to budget for **travel** within your new country of residence. Depending on how deep and how much you want to explore, you'll need to set aside some money in your budget for this.

As we get to the fringe of our budget planning, I recommend allotting money to **miscellaneous expenses** such as haircuts, manicures/pedicures, household expenses, dry cleaning, etc. Depending on where you choose to settle down, the miscellaneous expenses could amount for a very small or very big portion of your budget.

If you choose one of the countries from my wallet-friendly chapter (chapter 4) then your miscellaneous expenses will most likely be very low, however if you choose a country from the luxury chapter (chapter 5) then you'll probably need to allocate more money to this portion of your budget.

The biggest takeaway here is that you have a lot more control over your finances than you think. Once you define your budget and create a spreadsheet of how you'll allocate your money, it's very easy to stick to it. Living comfortably can look different to everyone and based on your budget, you'll be able to create your ideal "comfort". As mentioned early on in this chapter, your housing budget will be the primary expense to account for; and the biggest decision you'll make is "rent or buy?"

9. Renting or Buying a Home

The bulk of any budget will go into housing — whether you decide to rent or buy a home will define how much that "bulk" is!

My suggestion is that you rent for a minimum of 5 months to a year before committing to buying any property. Renting is the ideal situation to start — not only is it less of a commitment, but it also gives you a chance to figure out if you like living overseas or not.

You may think you love a certain place, move there, buy a home, only to realize a few months in that the place isn't what you hyped up to be at all. Now you're stuck with a home, a mortgage, and in a rush to sell while trying not to lose money. In order to avoid this from happening, I strongly urge you to start with a rental and then a year or so in you can reevaluate if you want to stay on and buy a home.

Housing will impact your cost of living drastically. If you choose to buy a home in a country where you're able to set up financing as an expat, you'll discover that your mortgage is barely more than your rent would be. However, if are choosing to own a home then you need to factor in repairs, maintenance, any type of house issues. You'll also need to factor in property taxes based on the country you're buying in, as well as homeowner's insurance, and groundskeeping costs if that's something you're interested in. It's important to note that these costs can add up, and as a renter you have none of these responsibilities and liabilities. So if buying seems like too much of a cost and responsibility then stick with renting!

Another thing to keep in mind is that depending on where you choose to settle down, your rent/house costs could be drastically effected. For example if you choose to settle down in a bigger city, with a nice building, pool, and doorman your rent will be a lot higher than if you choose to settle down in a little house near a beach or somewhere else remote. The country you choose is just as important as the area you choose within that country.

Because housing costs can vary enormously depending on a range of factors, the ideal way to create a budget is to itemize all the other expenses we discussed in the previous chapter. Once you've put together a rough amount based on the list from the previous chapter, you can figure out how much money you can truly put towards housing. Based on the amount you can delegate to housing, you can decide on a number of things — whether to rent or buy, whether to live near the beach or in the main city, and a number of other things.

Something else to keep in mind as a homeowner is the monthly condo/ homeowners association (HOA) fee. This fee is essentially your contribution to the costs of managing and maintaining your apartment/ community. It covers your share of the expenses required to keep the community you live in running. We have HOA fees back home in the US so it's pretty basic stuff and shouldn't surprise you too much.

These expenses include internal roads, paving, security, groundskeeping, upkeep of the swimming pool, gym, concierge, and other amenities. These expenses are something you will most likely deal with as both a renter and an owner. The HOA is referred to by different names in different countries, but the overall concept is the same. For example, in Panama this is called the *propiedad horizontal* fee and it refers to the cost of upgrading and managing public areas in apartment/ community complexes; these areas include elevators, pools, gyms, and game rooms. Similarly, in Paris the HOA fee is referred to as the syndic fee and it takes care of the cost of the lobby, elevator, courtyard, etc.

No matter where you are in the world this HOA fee is fairly common and therefore an important factor when creating your budget. While the HOA fee is typically expensed to the owner of the property, the fee is usually also bundled into the rent you pay. And for the most part, the HOA fee is primarily used for newer, more modern buildings with larger residential communities. It's not used as much for rentals for smaller, older buildings.

So as an owner and as a renter, this fee is important to think about and consider when figuring out your housing situation.

In addition to the HOA fee, another important consideration when putting together your housing budget, is property taxes. If you decide to buy over rent then property taxes will be an important expense to consider. Not all countries impose property taxes, for example Croatia doesn't. But it is important to note that most countries do impose property taxes. However, the property taxes you pay abroad will most likely be less than what you pay now at home in the US. This is because the percentage and/or value of the house is very likely less than real estate in the US. If you're renting then property taxes are something you wouldn't even have to think about.

As you can clearly see from this chapter, there are pros and cons to both renting and buying. Ultimately it all boils down to what's best for you and what suits your needs.

10. Shopping for the Best Health Insurance

Depending on where in the world you are, the cost of doctors and medical care in general can be a lot cheaper to pay out of pocket than by insuring against it. Additionally, in some places around the world, health care can even be free. In fact, more affordable health care is one of the biggest draws for American retirees looking to retire abroad.

The vast majority of countries around the world have more affordable healthcare than the US therefore one of the most popular reasons that people choose to retire overseas is this allure of a lower cost of living and access to affordable healthcare.

How you plan for health insurance and health care is by far one of the most intimate and important aspects of a retirement overseas. In your process of planning, you should first understand that your current local health insurance will most likely not carry over outside the US. Medicare, for example, definitely will not cover you abroad. So, wherever you move you will most likely need a new plan for health coverage.

You essentially have four options to choose from when setting up your medical insurance overseas.

Option 1. Purchase a domestic/local insurance policy; option 2. You could go for a travel insurance policy instead of health insurance. Option 3. Purchase an international insurance policy. And option 4. You could opt out of health insurance altogether and pay out of pocket instead. All four of these options have pros and cons; and the option you choose will depend on the country you're moving to, as well as the level of health coverage you're looking for.

The important thing to remember when shopping for your health insurance is that the option you choose depends on your individual circumstance and the country you're living in. Some countries are known to have great health care. For example Panama and Mauritius both have incredible and affordable health care. So in addition to their ocean views, warm weather, and tropical beaches, they also offer you great health insurance incentives.

Portugal also has great health care, which makes it a super desirable place to retire. Much like all of Europe, Portugal has a socialized health care system. And the biggest selling point here is that Portugal gives you access to this health care system when you become a legal resident. A lot of places in Europe have socialized health care — which is the most coveted type of health care. It essentially means that the government provides any and all aspects of health care. This includes employing health care providers, running health care facilities, and paying for all its citizens' healthcare.

An important fact to remember is that in most countries, local agencies will take you on as a new client only up to a certain age, the cut off is typically early to mid sixties. Similarly, most international insurance policies will take you on as a new client only if you're under the age of 75.

Cigna's international insurance policy, however, is one of the best and you can sign up for it as long as you're 80 or younger. The cost is certainly more than the others but depending on your needs, it may be the perfect policy for you and worth the roughly $200 USD a month. Once you're insured the coverage will take you through the rest of your life, granted you keep paying the premiums and monthly costs.

There's a whole bunch of options for International insurance but hands down my recommendation is Cigna. The coverage is amazing, the company is solid, and has been around forever, and will be here for a very long time! While a policy here is typically more expensive than a local insurance policy, the important thing to remember with Cigna and other international providers is that they work anywhere in the world.

So you can use them in the US, you can use them abroad, and if you're traveling around or choose to settle down somewhere new you can use it there too.

Here are the biggest questions you need to ask yourself as you begin shopping for health insurance:

1. Based on your needs and budget, would you prefer an international policy (ie. Cigna) or a local policy?

2. If you're planning on retiring only half-time/part-time to another country, would you prefer a travel insurance policy?

3. Would you rather opt out of health insurance altogether and pay out of pocket as needed?

Only you can weigh the level of risk with the level of money in order to come up with your ideal answer. While weighing the pros and cons of the different options, remember that local health insurance is usually cheap but restricted in its coverage. International insurance is typically more costly but covers you no matter where you choose to travel. Your decision will depend heavily on your present health status, age, and budget.

The vast majority of countries around the world have both private as well as public health care facilities. Public health care systems in developing countries typically have a lower standard of care than the US. This is why I highly recommend opting for private health care facilities. Regardless, here is the breakdown of the different insurance plans you can look into for yourself.

To start with, a **travel medical insurance** is the ideal option for you if you're looking for something quick, easy, and cheap. There's no extensive health history required so your coverage will be in effect almost immediately. If you'd like, there's also an option to get a $0 deductible, full coverage beyond a deductible (instead of paying a copay), and also you can become a new policyholder at pretty much any age (unlike international and local insurance that have age cutoffs for new policyholders).

Travel medical insurances are pretty much the most easy and flexible option for insurance. They're not designed to be long-term but they work well for the time they are used. They're a perfect option for those that are over the age limit for local and international insurances, and they're also a great option when you're trying out a new country but haven't fully committed to it yet.

To learn more about travel medical insurance and see if it's the right fit for you, check out: **www.insurancefortrips.com**

If travel medical insurance isn't quite the right option for you then perhaps you'd be more comfortable with a **hospital insurance plan**. The majority of countries give you the option to set up insurance through particular private hospitals. These types of hospital insurance plans are not a form of general health insurance, as they only take care of your treatment in the specific hospital you're assigned. If you're in need of medical care but are in another country or even in the same country but far away from the specific hospital that covers you, then you could find yourself in a really bad situation. You'll most likely wind up paying full costs at whatever hospital you are closest to.

Therefore, the hospital insurance plan is only good for retirees who are not looking to travel, who are settled down in a specific area of a specific country, and are committed to only receiving care from one hospital. These types of plans usually don't last too long and hospitals actually lose money with this plan and so they tend to not provide coverage under these plans for too long. The hospital insurance plans cater to very specific clients, and while there are a lot of drawbacks with it, there's also a lot of positives. These types of policies are super affordable (compared to other insurance options) and they also tend to include very attractive benefits. For example, in

Uruguay this type of plan is called a *mutualista* and costs only about $100 USD a month, which is a super affordable price for health insurance.

One of the most popular options is, of course, a **local medical insurance policy**. If you're planning on retiring abroad either full-time or part-time then this is one of the best options available. This insurance plan is perfect if you don't have any preexisting conditions and if you're under the age of 65. These insurance providers are usually attached to doctors and hospital networks throughout all countries, which means you're not tied to limited health care facilities and instead can receive care from a number of hospitals.

With this plan, your coverage will cover you anywhere within the country but not outside the country. If you're planning on traveling a lot then this plan probably isn't right for you; however, if you plan to stay local then this is the perfect plan for you. Local medical insurances are, for the most part, more reasonably priced than international insurance policies.

International medical insurance policies are the most expensive option but also the most dependable and most secure. If you're planning on retiring abroad full-time and you want to be as safe, secure, and medically-covered as possible then I strongly recommend getting an international medical insurance policy. For the most part, these policies bestow the most comprehensive and extensive care possible. They also provide the highest level of medical coverage.

With this plan, you don't need to depend on just one hospital or even just facilities in one country. You're covered at a global level! International medical insurance policies will protect you wherever you travel and for however long you remain there. These plans can however be very expensive and the premiums are set depending on your age and the level of coverage you're looking for.

The top companies for international medical insurance are Bupa, HTH Worldwide, and Cigna. HTH Worldwide is an option open only to Americans; it offers short-term travel medical insurance and annual plans for international living. Cigna offers a range of plans and each plan has flexibility with add-ons made available. Bupa is another great option if you're looking for great coverage that's also flexible.

As you go about trying to decide which option is best; remember, that depending on your situation what's best for you can be very different than what's best for someone else. Before planning your big move, it's vital that you figure out a health insurance plan and put your plan into effect as soon as possible.

11. Special Benefits for American Retirees

As an American citizen, you have a massive advantage. Countries across the world are competing for you; you're essentially the commodity that everyone wants. Think of yourself as the last size 9 at a shoe sale, and think of the hunger and desperation of those around you! Everyone wants US retirees and more importantly, their retirement income; and so, in order for this to happen, a number of countries across the globe have laid out attractive and alluring incentives to draw you in. These incentives come in the package of tax breaks, discounts, and a number of other perks. Some countries clearly offer more perks than others and this is demonstrated by the flock of American retirees headed to their sandy shores.

In the 1980s, Costa Rica decided to capitalize on American retirees and started a program to help lure in expats looking for a retirement destination. They started the very first program to target retired people; they called it the *pensionada* program, more commonly referred to as the "retired visa program". You qualified by simply meeting a minimum amount of retirement income. If you were able to meet this amount, then Costa Rica granted you the right to live in their country for as long as you pleased.

Since the genesis of this retirement program, many other places have created similar programs. These places include Ecuador, Panama, Uruguay, Colombia, Belize, the Dominican Republic, Argentina, and Mexico. American retirees bring in a lot of money, making them a huge commodity, this is why so many places are targeting Americans with these retirement visas. They're all trying to attract people like you, and in doing so they're offering amazing incentives and benefits!

While Costa Rice was in fact the very first to create the *pensionada* program, Panama was the one to expand and really capitalize on it. Therefore, **Panama** is one of the best places if you're looking for a place with special benefits. Their **pensionada** program offers a multitude of benefits for American retirees.

Panama immediately picked up where Costa Rica left off on the *pensionada* program. This program in Panama offers amazing in-country discounts for American retirees. Seniors, for example, receive half off on pretty much everything; from movies, doctors' visit, hotels, professional services, and more. Keep in mind that "seniors" in this instance applies to women over 55 and men over 60.

These discounts are super easy to get a hold off, and don't require a lot of time or energy. Keep in mind that Panama is already a fairly affordable place to live, so with these discounts it only get even more affordable. American retirees can peacefully live in Panama for under $3,000 USD a month. This includes utilities, rent, groceries, and even entertainment. Panama is also fairly close to the US making it easy to fly home for the holidays or even just fly back for nostalgia trips. There's also incredibly affordable health care, a reliable metro-system, amazing infrastructure, and well-paved roads here. Once you pair all that with the special benefits for American retirees, the ocean views, and the warm weather this becomes the number 1 spot for American retirees!

The pensionada program provides a number of special benefits, it also provides you with a visa to live here for as long as you'd like.

As an American retiree, you qualify for this program by having a pension of at least $1,000 USD a month and that's pretty much the only requirement there is.

The benefits that tag along with this *pensionada* program include half off all entertainment, this includes theaters, concerts, and movies. Given that you'll most likely be spending a fair amount fo time at these types of venues, 50% off is a huge steal! You also receive 30% off all public transport including boats, trains, and buses. The public transportation is super reliable and so having this discount makes it even easier to get around.

Other benefits under this program include: half off hotels, 25% off restaurants and airplane tickets, 15% off hospital bills, 20% off medical consults, and 25% off electric bills. These are just some of the benefits, there's so many more that you'll discover if you choose to live in Panama as a retiree.

Similar to Panama, **Belize** is also looking to shuffle in American retirees. Around 20 years ago, Belize allowed what they called "Qualified Retired People" (QRPs) to acquire permanent residency in the country. This led to massive flocks of retired people entering Belize! The QRP visa allows you to live here and enjoy the island life with a number of special benefits.

Belize not only offers a number of special incentives for retirees, but the country is also just beyond amazing. The laidback, peaceful, Caribbean lifestyle here is a massive draw for American retirees, especially considering there's no language barrier here, and the culture aligns beauti- fully with US culture.

Ambergris Caye is the largest island in Belize and is one of the most popular places that locals and expats choose to settle down. The downtown scene here is fun, lively, and is filled with beach bars and restaurants. Snorkeling, div- ing, and swimming are basically a lifestyle choice in Am- bergris Caye and so this is definitely the ideal retirement spot for you if you're looking for a tropical, fun retirement with special benefits targeting retirees like yourself.

If you like the idea of special benefits, island-life, and warm weather but you prefer a smaller, more quaint location then Hopkins is a great place to settle down. Hopkins is the smallest fishing village in Belize and has retained most of its seaside charm. The friendly people here will remind you of being back home.

Belize has capitalized on their beauty by adding in a number of incentives to draw American retirees in. Their QRP program offers basically our equivalent of a green card to all foreign retirees that are 45 and older. There's also a number of incentives under the QRP program such as immunity from paying all taxes in Belize, this includes estate tax, capital gains tax, income tax, household goods and automobile tax.

Saving this much money is a massive draw for American retirees who are looking to retire somewhere beautiful but also somewhere with reasonable pricing. Not only does Belize offer a low cost of living (via all their tax cuts) but Belize also has some of the most beautiful and well-known attractions in the world. For example, there's The Great Blue Hole — an ocean sinkhole ideal for divers; the Caracol Natural Monument — ruins of a sprawling Mayan city, The Belize Barrier Reef, and the Belize Zoo. Living here would ensure a number of benefits (primarily in the form of tax cuts) and a beautiful tropical retirement to top it off.

Another country, much like Belize, that has a number of special benefits for American retirees is **Malaysia**. Malaysia is one of the three countries in Asia that makes it easiest for Americans to retire in; the other two are the Philippines and Thailand.

To live in Malaysia on a permanent basis, American retirees can apply for what's called the "My Second Home" Program. To qualify for this program you need to show about $2,500 USD in annual income and have about $90,000 USD in assets. Because of this easy process, Malaysia is one of the most popular places that Americans choose to retire in Asia. In addition to the beneficial "My Second Home" Program, Malaysia also has a low cost of living, a phenomenal cuisine, tropical weather, and beautiful beaches. Malaysia is an excellent option if you've always wanted to live in Asia, but have a strict budget in place. Malaysia already has a well-formed expat community — with a lot of Americans choosing to retire in Penang.

Malaysia's "My Second Home" Program offers a number of tax cuts and other incentives for American retirees. This multiple-entry visa works for up to 10 years and even allows you to hold part-time employment in the country if that's something you're interested in. But the biggest benefit here is the tax status given to you by this visa. If you've qualified under the "My Second Home" Program then all your foreign-sourced income, including interest and pension, as well as foreign-earned income, is exempt from Malaysian taxes. This is a huge benefit that a lot of American retirees capitalize on when they move here!

The expat community is huge in Malaysia due to the tax benefits. The cities that have the biggest expat communities are Kuala Lumpur, Penang, Langkawi, and Malacca. Kuala Lumpur is the main hub in Malaysia — there's malls on every street corner, restaurants that cater to every cuisine, and a mix of the suburbs and city. Penang is a more traditional option — it has a very typical Southeast Asia vibe, and it's right by the water. You can easily find a villa or apartment with a sea-view in Penang, and there's a bunch of beaches all around.

Langkawi has more of a resort vibe to it, and is located in the Andaman Sea. It's great for those looking for a more remote and rural city. Malacca is less popular than the other 3 cities for retirement purposes; however, a lot of American retirees have found a happy home here. Malacca is located on the coast that divides Malaysia and Indonesia. It's a beautiful, tropical haven surrounded by water and good food.

All 4 of these cities are very popular with Americans as Malaysia has become a highly sought after retirement destination. In addition to the tax benefits mentioned above, Malaysia's "My Second Home" Program also offers a number of other benefits to American retirees. For example, as a member of this program you can import one automobile duty-free or buy a locally-made automobile free of sales tax and import duty.

Because of these types of benefits, a number of American retirees are flocking to Malaysia, Belize, and Panama. But before flocking here or to any of the other countries mentioned throughout this book, I strongly recommend reading my next chapter on overcoming cultural barriers. It's important to prepare yourself before diving in head-first into a new country and new culture.

12. Overcoming Cultural Barriers

You have to prepare yourself for some level of culture shock upon initial landing into your new country of residence. No matter how much prep-work you do and no matter how long you've scouted the plan prior to moving, there will still be a smidge (maybe even more) of culture shock. It's natural so try not to be scared or surprised by it. Culture shock can manifest itself differently for different people, and any seasoned expat will have their own unique story about how they first acclimated to the local culture.

The biggest thing to remember here is that any place you go is going to have its own way of doing things. Those ways will be different from what you've always know; those ways will frustrate you, confuse you, and at times drive you crazy. But for the sake of your mental wellbeing, you need to give up on the idea that "your way" or the "American way" is the right way! Every country and every culture will have its own unique approach and you need to remember, that's part of the overall experience of retiring overseas.

It's certainly easier to adjust to cultural differences if you have some idea of what you're getting into. Prior to my move to Singapore, I had visited the country a handful of times. My trips there had been weekly trips so I really got a sense and feel of the place. I understood the strict rules and efficiency of the country. I understood the culture, the diversity, and the foods. Therefore, when I did eventually move to Singapore the acclimation process was a lot easier than it would've been had I never visited before.

Sure, there was still an adjustment period; and of course, there were things that caught me by surprise. But the transition as a whole was a lot simpler thanks to the prep-work and visits I had put in place. This is why I strongly recommend visiting the place you plan to retire in before committing to anything. When I say "visit", I don't mean a week — I mean something closer to a month, maybe even two.

As I explained in chapter 3, living in any place for a month will give you a general idea of what living there longterm would look like. You may think the beach is for you until you realize the humidity isn't for you at all. You may love the idea of a sleepy town until you realize the town itself is lulling you to sleep when all you crave is excitement and adventure.

Our reality often has a way of not living up to our expectations; to avoid this let-down, we need to prepare as much as possible. A big part of this preparation is visiting our ideal destination and making sure that it is in fact — "ideal".

My ideal destination may look very different from your ideal destination. This is why creating a list of requirements prior to choosing a country can be very helpful. In order to avoid cultural barriers altogether, many Americans choose to retire in countries where there are no language or cultural barriers. I've highlighted this list of countries in chapter 7.

Chapter 7 will be massively helpful if the easiest course of action is what you're looking for. This chapter highlights countries that are a true home away from home. Countries that allow you to live in the tropics or the mountains but make you feel like you haven't traveled too far away. These countries have the same types of foods, background, languages, grocery stores, and products as the US. If you're looking for comfort but still want charm then you'd be happiest in countries that are most similar to the US, and have minimal cultural and language barriers.

As I explained earlier, I prepared heavily for my move from India to Singapore. However, my move from Singapore to the US required zero preparations. This move had zero cultural ramifications, as Singapore and the US are very similar. Both countries are proficient in English, have a deeply western background, have similar currencies, similar values. They even look, sound, and smell the same! Both Singapore and the US also believe deeply in diversity and in freedom of opinions and ideas, therefore there was no adjustment period and I was immediately able to adapt and blend in. I felt right at home and to this day, people are shocked to hear that I grew up in Singapore and not in the US.

Of course not all moves are this seamless and most countries will have very different cultural fabrics than the US. Therefore, preparing for the four stages of culture shock is a great approach when it comes to overcoming cultural barriers in any country.

Culture shock is simply a rollercoaster of emotions that we go through as we acclimate to a new culture. The first stage is typically: fascination. Much like relationships with people, we also develop a relationship with our new country of residence. Therefore, the very first stage of culture shock is fascination AKA the honeymoon stage. Everything, at first, seems interesting and exciting. We look at the differences in our new country as an adventure, a challenge, an exciting new endeavor.

However, this honeymoon stage doesn't last too long and you'll quickly find yourself in stage 2 of culture shock: frustration. During this stage, you'll take note of small daily irritations. It's also during this stage that you'll start noticing what you perceive as big differences between life back home and life in your new country. You'll notice yourself getting irked by these differences between your home country and your new country like differences in buying groceries and interacting with government officials. You'll get irritated with the communication differences, language barrier (if there is one). During this stage, you'll also start feeling resentment and hostility towards your new country of residence and you'll begin feeling homesick. The important thing to remember is that these feelings are completely natural and they will pass. Do not panic and buy a one-way ticket home; because, before you know it you'll be in stage 3 — acceptance.

During this third stage, you'll begin to realize your new life in this new country is in fact doable. You'll rebound from the homesickness, resentment, and frustration and begin to feel a sense of ease and a feeling of "I can do this". You'll begin to accept that your new country is different, and maybe even come to like some of those differences. During this stage, understanding breeds into acceptance; which takes us to step 4 — enjoyment.

This is the stage when your new country of residence begins feeling like a real home. The small differences and annoyances you once deemed to be important may matter less or you may have even grown to like them. During this stage, your neighbors have turned into friends, you've learned some of the local language, you've found a favorite restaurant, you know where the best shopping is, and which beaches are less crowded on weekends. You've really begin to learn about the country, the culture, the people, and why things work the way they do. It's during this stage that you fall in love with your new way of life, and remember why you made this move in the first place.

These four stages are a rough diagram of what your retirement may look like when you first move abroad, but within time the culture shock will wear off and you will begin to settle into your new life.

13. Settling Into Your New Life

Once you've made it through the four stages of culture shock and overcome the initial cultural barriers, you'll begin to feel a lot more confident in your new country and in your new life.

You'll begin to develop an ease — an ease with your new routine, an ease with your new community, and an ease with your new mentality. Things that initially seemed scary will begin to fade, as will some of the stress and homesickness.

Settling into your new life overseas begins with you allowing your new home to become a real home. Whether you chose to rent, buy, renovate, or build this home. Whether it's in the city, by the sea, up in the mountains, tucked away in a fishing village, or in a town. It doesn't matter. What matters is that this home isn't just any home, it's your home. While it may be difficult to avoid comparing it to the home you left behind, it's important that you don't do play this comparison game. Try instead to make an entirely fresh start by taking a positive outlook. Avoid saying phrases like "back home" and instead find ways to bring a sense of beauty and comfort to your new home.

What might help make your new home feel like a real home is developing a relationship with your community, and maybe even learning the local language and making a few friends. Interacting with the people around you will instantly make your feel more comfortable and at ease in your new surroundings. Not knowing anyone in your new country of residence and not making the effort to get to know anyone, can really slow you down. It'll take you a lot longer to accomplish things if you don't make that initial effort; things like setting up an office, establishing housekeeping, finding your way around, and finding the best restaurants are a lot easier if you have people around you helping and advising.

The better connected you are in your new home, the easier it is to navigate and settle in. This connection is built in two phases. The first phase begins before you even move overseas. It begins by scouting the place you plan to retire in before actually retiring there! Visiting and living in any place for a month will give you a general idea of what living there longterm will look like. Our reality often has a way of not living up to our expectations; to avoid this let-down, we need to prepare as much as possible. A big part of this preparation is visiting our ideal destination and making sure that it is in fact — "ideal".

Once you've visited and really lived in the place and you're now committed, you move there. At this point, you can begin phase 2 of the connection. Phase 2 is becoming a part of the community and making friends.

You begin this phase by first asking yourself the following question: What are your favorite hobbies and what do you like to do in your free time? Whatever your favorite hobby is, take time to find like-minded enthusiasts in your new home. If you're interested in gardening, join a gardening cub; if tennis is your outlet then buy all-white and join a country club; if art calls your name then take local art courses and maybe even a "paint and sip" (classes where you drink wine while painting). No matter what your passion and hobbies are, if you make the effort to seek out like-minded enthusiasts, you will find them and you will build a new circle of friends in your new home. The best part is these friends won't just be acquaintances that you have zero in common with. You'll have an activity and a hobby you share with them, so you can spend long days together and still have plenty to talk about.

Most countries also have expat organizations that are always on the lookout for new members. In Singapore, we had the IWC (International Women's Club). The club was filled with women from all over; they represented America, France, Germany, and the UK. These club meetings were conducted on a biweekly basis and really allowed the women to meet like-minded individuals who were in the same boat as them. Making friends through international organizations such as these and through activities that you enjoy is a great start to building connections!

It's also a good idea to get to know your neighbors and the other locals around you; hang out where they do, eat at the local restaurants, or go for a drink at the local pub. Learn some of the local language — I don't expect you to become conversational (unless of course you want to) but at least take time to learn some of the basic phrases. A few essential words will be enough to get your started, and if you're interested in learning more and refining your vocabulary you could always join classes where you can maybe meet even more friends!

Simple phrases like "hello" or "today's a warm day" will be great conversation starters for the locals and will get you some nice smiles and waves. Once you've made some friends, built a real community around you, and taken the time to decorate your home you'll begin feeling a lot more settled into your new life.

At this point it's important to settle in even further by making it a point to get out and about. Explore your new town, your new city. See what the people there do, watch how they spend their time, and where they eat. Stop in at the local shops and linger at the cafes. Little by little, get to know your new home and once you're comfortable enough, maybe even take a day trip or a weekend get-away to a nearby beach, park, or mountain range.

No matter where in the world you end up, the lifestyle you enjoy will be solely dependent on you. You decide how much effort you want to put into carving out a new life and you decide how much enjoyment you'll reap from that effort.

When we first moved to Tokyo, I was giddy with excitement — I had always dreamed of living in a place like Tokyo; and when we moved there, I made the most of it. Part of the reason my experience in Tokyo was so full and rich was because I chose to make it that way. It took me time to get acclimated to the Japanese culture, but I made the effort and put in the time. I indulged and fully submerged myself into Tokyo.

Known for its Harajuku fashion, beautiful temples, sky-scrapers that meet the clouds, and cherry blossom trees that color the streets below; Tokyo is every travelers dream. I made sure to fulfill my "Tokyo dream" by getting to know the best people, the best places, and the best restaurants. Living there taught me that most of the simple pleasures really are free but you need to invest the time in finding these pleasures!

While there are so many pleasures and benefits to living overseas, at times it can be challenging and frustrating; which is why it's important to manage your expectations and learn how to deal with the fear of being somewhere new.

14. Managing Expectations & Dealing with Fear

When moving abroad, it helps massively if you maintain some perspective and remove the rose-tinted glasses. For example, it helps to remember that Belize is a country in the Caribbean and while its sandy beaches are beautiful, they also sometimes swarm with insects. Madrid and Barcelona are lovely and spirited, but they're also in Spain and therefore the people in this country primarily speak Spanish.

It's important that no matter where in the world you're planning to retire, you think not only of all the good things, but also remember that there will be bad. While it's natural to build something up in your head and to have the highest expectations as you embark on a new adventure, it's important to dial some of this back. While it's obviously impossible to suppress all our expectations, it is important to keep a clear head as we navigate and create our retirement plan.

The most vital thing in managing your expectations is first understanding your motive in the first place. Why do you want to retire overseas? There are a number of reasons to choose from. One of the most popular reasons that people choose to retire overseas is the allure of a lower cost of living and access to affordable healthcare. A lot of countries have a far lower cost of living than the U.S, as was discussed in chapter 4. These countries also tend to have access to more affordable healthcare, as was detailed in chapter 8.

A lower cost of living is just one of the many reasons people choose to retire overseas. Other common reasons include better weather, retiree incentives, change in scenery, or making a reality out of a dream. There's emotional reasons to retire overseas and there's also logical, pragmatic reasons. But no matter what your reason is, it's a decision you can't go wrong with as long as you've thought it through and done the appropriate research.

It's important to outline your retirement plan so that you know exactly why you're making this move and why it's worth it you. By knowing why it's worth it, you avoid (or at the very least, diminish) feelings of fear, resentment, worry, and doubt in the longterm. This is why the most important thing to do before you retire overseas is to make sure you're doing it for the right reasons, and having those reasons clearly laid out in your mind. If you're not committed to the idea of moving abroad, chances are it won't work out. As I said in chapter 1, commitment doesn't mean there shouldn't be any feelings of fear or sadness, it simply means that in your mind the good outweighs the bad and you feel ready for this move.

This commitment will not only help fight feelings of fear and doubt, but it'll also help you keep a level-head. It'll help you manage your expectation so that when you do land in your desired country, you're keeping your mind and your heart open to the good, the bad, the ugly, and the beautiful.

In addition to being sure in our decision, it's also important to get input from others. Talking to people who have experienced an international move in some capacity really helps to manage expectations and make things more realistic. These people can provide interesting and helpful ideas and tips. It's important when gaining insight from others that you listen to the opinions you don't agree with as much as the ones you do agree with. For example if you've pictured Paris to be a specific way (ie. romantic and friendly) and you consult with someone who lived there for many years and he says that the culture in Paris was very hostile. Then, it's important that you take that input into consideration. It doesn't necessarily mean that your experience will be the same as his, and it also doesn't mean that you should no longer move to Paris.

But all I am saying is that it's important to think about these more negative things and to reflect on if there's any truth to them. If you only take in the good information and the information you agree with, then your confirmation bias will clog your vision and leave you with unrealistic expectations of a place. Instead, it's a much better approach to listen to those around you and to prepare yourself for whatever may come.

No matter how well you manage your expectations and prepare yourself, you will feel some level of fear and panic. It's entirely natural so don't let it worry you too much. Thoughts that will most likely fill your hand early on and at times throughout your stay will sound like this: "what was I thinking?" "was I out of my mind?" "this place isn't paradise, it's a nightmare."

This thought stream is completely natural and no matter how much preparation you put into the move, you cannot avoid these thoughts. No matter how ready and excited you were for this move, at some point during the first year you will absolutely wonder why you moved and whether it was the right decision for you. The important thing here to help fight off this fear is to remember that no matter how strong these feelings and thoughts may seem, they are fleeting and therefore will pass at some point.

The key to dealing with the fear and finding your happiness is to maintain your perspective, as previously discussed, and also to find a sense of humor about the things that would otherwise upset you. When fear and doubt creep in, as they always do, it's important to remind yourself of two things.

First, don't make any swift, sweeping decisions. This moment of fear will pass. And second, while you're waiting for the fear to pass, remind yourself why you chose this country and this home in the first place. Was it because of the beautiful white-sand beach? If it was; then, in that moment choose to escape to the ocean for a few days. Was it because of the low cost of living? If it was, then take yourself out for a nice, cheap meal and enjoy! Whatever it is that you enjoy most about your new country and whatever it is that drew you here in the first place is ultimately what will keep you here.

You should also think about why, in this moment, you're feeling fear and doubt. No place is perfect so once you zoom in and identify the negatives of the place and why they're getting you down, you can figure out a way to get past them. If you don't like the current season you're stuck in, travel somewhere new till it passes. If you're nostalgic and missing your family then invite them to come see you. If the neighborhood you're in makes you unhappy then do some research and find a better one.

The point is that if you're considering making a reality out of your dream by retiring overseas then by all means, do it! Believe in yourself, take your chance; but be prepared that you will have doubts early on, you will have fear and unease. In those moments you need to remind yourself why you moved out here in the first place. Eventually, the fear will pass, and on the other side of that fear is the life you came to find.

15. Conclusion: Lessons I've Learned Living Abroad

I was born in India so my first experience abroad was in Singapore. I then became a Singaporean citizen so my second experience abroad was in Tokyo, Japan. Shortly after Tokyo, I moved to the US. I've now been here for almost 10 years. First in Pennsylvania and now in New Jersey. I can confidently say New Jersey is now my home. While I am technically living abroad, I've never felt more at home and more like myself.

My move from India to Singapore was not an easy one emotionally. I was terrified to leave the bustling city of New Delhi for the tall skylines peppered with beaches and palm trees. I was terrified of leaving behind the friends I grew up with, the smells I had grown accustomed to, and the memories I had created.

But like I mentioned earlier, Singapore did begin to feel like home and it became my home for many many years. I loved it so much that I eventually got citizenship here. There were many things I loved about it. I loved living in a country where the beach was as close to you as the mall was. A country that was as rich in culture as it was in money. A country where the food court at the mall was as gourmet as any 5-star restaurant. I fell in love with the culture, the colors, the smells, and the vibrant nature that made this country what it was.

There are so many reasons to move to a foreign country, and the point in telling you my story is that no matter how scary this move might be, you will grow to love the place you move to as much as the place you moved from. Maybe even more. If my experience as an expat has taught me anything, it's taught me that a home can be built anywhere, as long as you're surrounded by joy and love.

Living abroad and creating new homes has also taught me that you can't plan everything. While it's incredibly important to review budgets, outline ideas, and make proposals, you cannot plan for the emotions and the heart of it all. Once you've finally arrived in your new country, in your new life, you need to let your heart take over. When you let that happen there's no telling how visceral, how strong your attachment to the place will become.

Tokyo was the most magical place I've ever lived. A romantic bubble blended with adventure, beauty, tranquility, and peace. There were nights where I would sit on my balcony overlooking twinkling lights, tall skyscrapers and simply reminisce on how lucky I was to be living in this magical city. Sipping my Sauvignon Blanc, I had visions of staying here forever, I truly never wanted to leave.

When I did eventually move to the U.S. I realized that I had forever left a piece of myself in Tokyo. I also realized that I've felt this way about a number of places. Every time I leave somewhere beautiful, somewhere magical, I feel as though I'm leaving behind a piece of myself. South Africa, Russia, Paris, New Zealand, Singapore, no matter where I had gone or how long I had been there, a part of me was changed and a part of me was left behind.

While I miss all these amazing places, New Jersey is now — without a shadow of a doubt — the best home I've ever had. Moving here, living here as an expat, was the best decision I ever made.

It's not something I can quantify and answer scientifically. While there's certainly a list of reasons why I love it here, what it ultimately boils down to is the feeling of the place. I connect with it. So while my book has certainly approached the "how to retire overseas" question very scientifically through lists, comparisons, pros and cons, in the end, the choice to launch your retirement overseas is just as emotional as it is financial and pragmatic.

This is why the most important part of the process, as I've been explaining, is to hop on a plane and get a sense of the place you'd like to retire in before making your final decision. This type of soul-searching is so important in order to understand what you're looking for in your retirement abroad. Really take the time, if you can, to identify the pros and cons of the places that appeal to you the most. Plan an extended stay in these places and get a true sense of them. See if the place speaks to you. No amount of planning or reading can do this part for you, it's purely feeling-based. You need to walk the streets, hangout with the people, watch the waves crash into rocks, and the sunsets melt away. You'll immediately notice what places speak to you, what places feel safe and welcoming, and what places don't.

We live in a big, beautiful, messy, wonderful world filled with opportunities for excitement and adventure, so be sure to really explore all the wonder before narrowing down on one place! Once you have narrowed it down to that one place and you've moved there and you're building a new home, you will need to learn the art of patience. It's something that I've certainly learned about living as an expat. This is a crucial lesson that pertains specifically to parts of the world that move at a slower pace. Living in the U.S. has engrained into us this feeling of "move, move, move" and with that we expect quick delivery, quick service. We're always on the move, always on the hunt.

But the whole beauty of moving abroad and living somewhere tropical or mountainous is slowing down. What you need to expect with this new pace of life is that everything will most likely move slower in your new country of residence. Service at restaurants, dealing with government officials, checkout lines at the grocery store, package deliveries, etc. You need to accept this; and therefore, you need to learn the art of patience, just like I did!

Another lesson I've learned from living abroad is that you have to be willing to embrace the unknown and lean towards the feeling of newness. The only way you're going to truly flourish in your new life is if you accept that you can't control or predict everything. You may arrive with a certain list of ideas, but you'll throw pretty much all of that out the window once you actually begin the acclimation process. When you first arrive in your new country of residence everything will be a mystery and most things will take a lot of trial and error to figure out. Lean into this feeling of doubt, of newness and really allow yourself to be okay with not controlling every aspect of your experience.

A large part of giving up your sense of control means relying on the things and the people around you — which leads me to the next lesson I've learned in my time overseas: it's important to ask for help. You may want to figure it all out for yourself and not rely on anyone, but that's a terrible attitude to have! By leaning on the people close to you, you not only get around easier but you also form a nice community and circle of friends in the process.

This leads me to the final lesson I've learned in my time abroad, and I can sum it up pretty easily for you: take the leap! No matter how scared you are, no matter how daunting it may all seem, if it's something you really want for yourself then you simply have to do it. Worst thing that happens? You try it, don't like, and return home. But at least you'll know you tried instead of sitting there and always wondering "what if".

If you're going back and forth on where to go and can't figure out where the "right" place is; then remember, there is no right place. Trying out difference places is part of the adventure! You may be worried that you're too old or too young, too inexperienced or too attached to your routine. You may be worried about settling in or feeling out of place. But I promise you, none of these worries are worth pushing aside a dream and a chance to discover a new way of life. So, get up, get moving.

Your freedom begins now; how will you spend it?

Reviews

Reviews and feedback help improve this book and the author. If you enjoy this book, we would greatly appreciate it if you could take a few moments to share your opinion and post a review on Amazon.